The Caroling

MW00811522

This book is about the economy of the Carolingian empire (753–877), which extended from the Pyrenees and the northern shores of the Mediterranean to the North Sea, and from the Atlantic coast to the Elbe and Saale rivers. It is the first comprehensive evaluation of the topic in English in over twenty years.

The study of the Carolingian empire as an economic rather than a political entity can be justified both because of the major interference of political authority in the economy, and because of the distinctive economic characteristic of growth; and while some regions within the empire had a much more developed economy than others, the whole period is basically one of economic expansion, in parallel with the cultural upheaval of the 'Carolingian Renaissance'.

This economic and cultural flowering raises the question of its causes – and of its limits. Moreover, this positive evaluation contrasts with the generally accepted idea of the Carolingian period as lacking in commerce and dominated by a purely agrarian economy. By contrast, this book aims to show not only the diversified agrarian roots of Carolingian society, but also their significance for manufacture, industry and commerce.

ADRIAAN VERHULST is Emeritus Professor of Medieval Economic History, University of Ghent. His publications include *The Rise of Cities in North-West Europe* (Cambridge, 1999).

Cambridge Medieval Textbooks

This is a series of specially commissioned textbooks for teachers and students, designed to complement the monograph series Cambridge Studies in Medieval Life and Thought by providing introductions to a range of topics in medieval history. This series combines both chronological and thematic approaches, and will deal with British and European topics. All volumes in the series will be published in hard covers and in paperback.

For a list of titles in the series, see end of book.

THE CAROLINGIAN ECONOMY

ADRIAAN VERHULST

CAMBRIDGE
UNIVERSITY PRESS

PUBLISHED BY THE PRESS SYNDICATE OF THE UNIVERSITY OF CAMBRIDGE
The Pitt Building, Trumpington Street, Cambridge, United Kingdom

CAMBRIDGE UNIVERSITY PRESS
The Edinburgh Building, Cambridge CB2 2RU, UK
40 West 20th Street, New York, NY 10011-4211, USA
477 Williamstown Road, Port Melbourne, VIC 3207, Australia
Ruiz de Alarcón 13, 28014 Madrid, Spain
Dock House, The Waterfront, Cape Town 8001, South Africa

http://www.cambridge.org

First published 2002

Printed in the United Kingdom at the University Press, Cambridge

Typeface Bembo 10.75/12.5 pt   *System* LATEX 2$_\varepsilon$ [TB]

A catalogue record for this book is available from the British Library

ISBN 0 521 80869 3 hardback
ISBN 0 521 00474 8 paperback

To the memory of François-L. Ganshof

CONTENTS

_____ • _____

INTRODUCTION

—————— • ——————

The title of this book needs some explanation. 'Carolingian economy' has to be understood here as 'the economy of the Carolingian empire'. The 'economy of the Carolingian period' would be too broad, not being limited to the empire within its borders under Charlemagne, which is the point of view adopted here. Countries and regions outside the empire, such as England, Scandinavia, the Islamic empire (including the bigger part of Spain), the Byzantine empire and eastern Europe, will be considered only in so far as their commercial relations with the Carolingian empire are at stake. The chronological terms, from the middle of the eighth century to the end of the ninth, are necessarily political, but they coincide by chance with the beginning and the end of an economic period, as will be demonstrated in Chapter 10. 'Carolingian economy' can also be understood as an economy directed by the Carolingian rulers. I do not reject this interpretation altogether, but it will be elucidated in Chapter 9 on 'The economy and the state'. 'Economy' is used in its singular form although the Carolingian empire was not an economically homogeneous area. Several regional 'economies' can be defined, each having different characteristics regarding population, the use of money, the presence of towns, the intensity of trade, etc. The territories between the Loire and the Rhine, between the Rhine and the frontier of the empire on the Elbe river and northern Italy are the most striking examples. Nevertheless an inquiry into the specificity of the Carolingian economy as a whole, compared with regions outside the empire or to economic situations before and after the Carolingian period, makes sense and is possible. Was it, to quote Chris Wickham,[1] 'a network of subsistence-based exchange', where consumption commanded production, or was it an economy producing surpluses brought to the market?

This alternative comes near to that of Pirenne, for whom the Carolingian economy was a closed agrarian-based economy without towns, merchants or trade. His views, most strikingly expressed in his book *Mahomet et Charlemagne* (completed after his death in 1935 and published, with documentary evidence by his pupil Fernand Vercauteren, in 1937),[2] were essentially a reaction to ideas advanced by Alfons Dopsch in the second edition (1921–2) of his two-volume book, written between 1911 and 1913, on the economic evolution of the Carolingian period (*Die Wirtschaftsentwicklung der Karolingerzeit*).[3] In this book Dopsch had reacted against the conceptions of what he calls the old nineteenth-century school of von Inama-Sternegg and Karl Lamprecht, who had proclaimed the primacy of the manor ('Grundherrschaft') in Carolingian economic life. Opposing their views on an agrarian-based economy, Dopsch stressed the role of towns, money and trade. This point of view might have been expected from Pirenne but he, paradoxically, just took the side of the old school, where Lamprecht, before the First World War, had been his model and closest friend. It is however not the place here to enter into the genesis of Pirenne's *Mahomet et Charlemagne*,[4] but rather to review the historiography since Pirenne on the economic evolution under the Carolingians.

The first phase of this historiography, from the late 1930s through to the 1950s, was driven by an attack on Pirenne's work and, in particular, his thesis about the role of the Arabs. The absolute masters of the western Mediterranean since 711, they had, according to Pirenne, forced the western Christian world to retreat to the north from what until then had remained the centre of the civilised world, imposing a continental character on the Carolingian empire. In this way it put an

---

[1] Chris Wickham, *Land and Power. Studies in Italian and European Social History, 400–1200* (London, 1994), p. 197.

[2] Henri Pirenne, *Mohammed and Charlemagne*, English translation (London, Unwin, 1939). Paperback edition by Barnes and Noble (New York, 1955).

[3] Alfons Dopsch, *Die Wirtschaftsentwicklung der Karolingerzeit vornehmlich in Deutschland*, second revised edition, 2 vols. (Weimar, 1921–2).

[4] Paolo Delogu, 'Reading Pirenne Again' in Richard Hodges and William Bowden (eds.), *The Sixth Century. Production, Distribution and Demand* (Leiden, Brill, 1998), pp. 15–40.

end to the circulation, mostly by Syrian merchants, from the shores of the Mediterranean to the north, of goods such as papyrus, spices, oriental wines and olive oil. Different studies re-examined the references to these products in Merovingian and Carolingian texts and concluded that their disappearance from Carolingian texts had never been so complete nor so early as Pirenne had believed or had had other causes.[5]

More fundamental than the discussions on documentary evidence for the presence of these goods, was the argument about the causes of the adoption by the Carolingians of the silver penny and their abandonment of gold coins, which Pirenne had also related to the Arab conquest of the western Mediterranean and to the economic regression which in his opinion had been its consequence in the west.

In the late 1940s and early 1950s Maurice Lombard developed a theory about the vast quantities of gold the Arabs had acquired through conquest in Persia and Africa and which they brought into circulation. With this gold, according to Lombard, they bought slaves, wood, furs and other wares in western Europe and vivified its economy.[6] Sture Bolin supported these unorthodox views but through different ways, tracing trade links between the Arab lands and Scandinavia that would explain the hoards of Arab silver coins found in Scandinavia which finally reached western Europe.[7] These theories did not stand firm: Grierson proved that no Arab gold coins circulated in western Europe in any significant quantities.[8] Moreover most of the Arabic coins found in Birka (near Stockholm, Sweden) date from the end of the ninth century and the beginning of the tenth,[9] although a hoard of several thousand Arabic silver coins, the latest

[5] Bryce Lyon, *The Origins of the Middle Ages. Pirenne's Challenge to Gibbon* (New York, 1972), pp. 70–6.

[6] Maurice Lombard, 'Les bases monétaires d'une suprématie économique. L'or musulman du VIIe au XIe siècle', *Annales. Economies–Sociétés–Civilisations* 2 (1947), pp. 143–60; Maurice Lombard, 'Mahomet et Charlemagne. Le problème économique', *Annales. Economies–Sociétés–Civilisations* 3 (1948), pp. 188–99.

[7] Sture Bolin, 'Mohammad, Charlemagne and Ruric', *The Scandinavian Economic History Review* 1 (1953), pp. 5–39.

[8] Philip Grierson, 'Carolingian Europe and the Arabs: The Myth of the Mancus', *Revue belge de philologie et d'histoire* 32 (1954), pp. 1059–74.

[9] Björn Ambrosiani, 'Excavations in the Black Earth Harbour 1969–71', in Björn Ambrosiani and Helen Clarke (eds.), *Early Investigations and Future Plans*, Birka Studies 1 (Stockholm, 1992), p. 79.

dating from the mid-ninth century, was concealed at Ralswiek, on
the island of Rügen, off the north-German Baltic coast.[10] This does
not mean that there was no direct commerce between the Arab world
and western Europe in Carolingian times, as Pirenne, not without
admitting some exceptions, notably concerning the slave trade, contended. But their economic impact must not be exaggerated, even
if Grierson himself and other numismatists suppose a link between
the Carolingian monetary reform of the mid-eighth century and an
earlier Arab reform at the end of the seventh century.[11] Numismatic
evidence, which in this case too is scanty, does not indeed, in the
opinion of K. F. Morrison, tell anything certain about trade routes or
about the volume of trade.[12] On the basis of documentary evidence
however, F.-L. Ganshof, himself a disciple of Pirenne, demonstrated
the year after *Mahomet et Charlemagne* had appeared, that in the eighth
century the relations between East and West continued through the
ports of Provence, particularly in Marseilles, be it on a minimal
level.[13] H. L. Adelson has made Byzantium responsible for this state of
affairs[14] and other authors also tried to prove that relations between
the West and Byzantium and the East, mainly through Italian ports
under theoretical Byzantine authority, like Venice and Tyrrenean
ports in southern Italy, particularly Amalfi, depended in the first place
on the military relations between Byzantium and the Arabs in the
eastern Mediterranean.

As the essential part of Pirenne's thesis, the negative role of the
Arabs, with as its consequences the absence of merchants, towns
and trade in western Europe and the predominance of an agrarian economy based on the self-sufficiency of the big estate, has
been rejected totally or partially by most of his critics, only the latter element, in a second phase of the historiography of Pirenne's
critics, has been the object of new studies. That the attention shifted
from trade to agriculture may be explained by the satiation caused

[10] Helen Clarke and Björn Ambrosiani, *Towns in the Viking Age*, second revised
edition (London: Leicester University Press, 1995), p. 109.
[11] Philip Grierson, 'The Monetary Reforms of Abd-Al-Malik', *Journal of Economic
and Social History of the Orient*, 3 (1960), pp. 241–64.
[12] Karl F. Morrison, 'Numismatics and Carolingian Trade: A Critique of the
Evidence', *Speculum* 38 (1963), p. 432.
[13] François-L. Ganshof, 'Note sur les ports de Provence du viiie au xe siècle', *Revue
Historique* 184 (1938), pp. 28–37.
[14] H. L. Adelson, 'Early Medieval Trade Routes', *American Historical Review*
65 (1960), pp. 271–87.

by the numerous critics during the first historiographical phase, all centred on trade, and the paradoxical situation that in his *Mahomet et Charlemagne* Pirenne himself had been very brief on the role of the manor, although he considered it the basis of the Carolingian economy. The prelude to the second historiographical phase in the 1950s and early 1960s, besides the roneotyped but important lectures by Charles-Edmond Perrin at the Sorbonne, was several fundamental studies by two German scholars, K. Verhein and W. Metz, on the sources for the study of the royal Carolingian estates, more particularly a capitulary of Charlemagne known as the *Capitulare de Villis* and inventories known as *Brevium exempla*.[15] To this phase belonged the 1965 'Settimana' in Spoleto on agriculture in the early Middle Ages, where I presented a new thesis on the origin of the classical bipartite estate, so typical for the Carolingian period. Its development in the eighth to ninth centuries was on the model of the royal estates between the Seine and the Rhine.[16]

Although my views were widely accepted, the real start of manorial studies centred on the Carolingian period were three international colloquia respectively held in Xanten (1980), Ghent (1983) and Göttingen (1987).[17] At Xanten I counted 109 studies published between 1965 and 1980 on that particular topic while Yoshiki Morimoto in 1988 numbered a hundred new titles between 1980 and 1986.[18] Meanwhile, at the Göttingen Academy, on the initiative of the archaeologist Herbert Jankuhn, a series of colloquia on the material

[15] Klaus Verhein, 'Studien zu den Quellen zum Reichsgut der Karolingerzeit', *Deutsches Archiv für Erforschung des Mittelalters* 10 (1954), pp. 313–94 and 11 (1955), pp. 333–92; Wolfgang Metz, *Das Karolingische Reichsgut* (Berlin 1960).

[16] Adriaan Verhulst, 'La genèse du régime domanial classique en France au haut moyen âge', reprinted in Adriaan Verhulst, *Rural and Urban Aspects of Early Medieval Northwest Europe* (Aldershot: Variorum, 1992).

[17] Walter Janssen and Dietrich Lohrmann (eds.), *Villa – Curtis – Grangia. Landwirtschaft zwischen Loire und Rhein von der Römerzeit zum Hochmittelalter. 16. Deutschfranzösisches Historikerkolloquium, Xanten 1980* (Munich, 1983); Adriaan Verhulst (ed.), *Le grand domaine aux époques mérovingienne et carolingienne. Actes du colloque international Gand 1983* (Ghent, 1985); Werner Rösener (ed.), *Strukturen der Grundherrschaft im frühen Mittelalter* (Göttingen, 1989).

[18] Yoshiki Morimoto, 'Etat et perspectives des recherches sur les polyptyques carolingiens', *Annales de l'Est* 5–40 (1988), pp. 99–149; for the years 1987–1992: Yoshiki Morimoto, 'Autour du grand domaine carolingien: aperçu critique des recherches récentes sur l'histoire rurale du Haut Moyen Âge (1987–92)', in Adriaan Verhulst and Yoshiki Morimoto (eds.), *L'économie rurale et l'économie urbaine au Moyen Âge* (Ghent, Fukuoka, 1994), pp. 25–79.

and archaeological aspects of prehistoric and early medieval agriculture began in 1977.[19] In the 1980s, a 'boom' of critical editions put at the disposal of specialists the annotated texts of nearly all the preserved Carolingian polyptychs and inventories: those of the abbeys of Prüm, Wissembourg (Weissenburg), Montiérender, St Maur-des-Fossés and last but not least St Germain-des-Prés, mostly at the initiative of Dieter Hägermann from Bremen University and all by German scholars.[20] Before that Belgian scholars had published other famous Carolingian polyptychs and inventories, namely F.-L. Ganshof that of St Bertin, J.-P. Devroey those of Reims and Lobbes and I myself a fragment of a Carolingian inventory of St Bavo's at Ghent.[21]

After this 'boom' of studies on Carolingian manorial organisation, which even touched Italy,[22] there was a need for evaluation and synthesis, especially as Robert Fossier in a fuss-making pamphlet at the 1979 'Settimana' in Spoleto had passed a very negative judgement on Carolingian economy.[23] Nearly ten years later, in 1988, a confrontation with Fossier was organised at the abbey of Flaran under

[19] Herbert Jankuhn, Rudolf Schützeichel and Fred Schwind (eds.), *Das Dorf der Eisenzeit und des frühen Mittelalters* (Göttingen: Abhandlungen der Akademie der Wissenschaften, 1977); Heinrich Beck, Dietrich Denecke and Herbert Jankuhn (eds.), *Untersuchungen zur eisenzeitlichen und frühmittelalterlichen Flur in Mitteleuropa und ihrer Nutzung* (Göttingen: Abhandlungen der Akademie der Wissenschaften, 1979–80).

[20] Ingo Schwab (ed.), *Das Prümer Urbar* (Düsseldorf, 1983); Christoph Dette (ed.), *Liber possessionum Wizenburgensis* (Mainz, 1987); Claus-Dieter Droste (ed.), *Das Polytichon von Montierender* (Trier, 1988); Dieter Hägermann and Andreas Hedwig (eds.), *Das Polyptychon und die Notitia de Areis von Saint-Maur-des-Fossés* (Sigmaringen, 1989); Dieter Hägermann, Konrad Elmshäuser and Andreas Hedwig (eds.), *Das Polyptychon von Saint-Germain-des-Prés* (Cologne, Weimar, Vienna, 1993).

[21] François-L. Ganshof (ed.), *Le polyptyque de l'abbaye de Saint-Bertin (844–859)* (Paris, 1975); Jean-Pierre Devroey (ed.), *Le polyptyque et les listes de cens de l'abbaye de Saint-Remi de Reims (IXe–XIe siècles)* (Reims, 1984); Jean-Pierre Devroey (ed.), *Le polyptyque et les listes de biens de l'abbaye Saint-Pierre de Lobbes (IXe–XIe siècles)* (Brussels, 1986); Adriaan Verhulst, 'Das Besitzverzeichnis der Genter Sankt-Bavo-Abtei von ca 800 (Clm 6333)', *Frühmittelalterliche Studien* 5 (1971), pp. 193–234.

[22] Pierre Toubert, 'L'Italie rurale aux VIIIe–IXe siècles. Essai de typologie domaniale', in *I problemi dell'Occidente nel secolo VIII* (Spoleto, 1973: Settimane di studio del Centro italiano di studi sull'alto medioevo 20), pp. 95–132; Bruno Andreolli and Massimo Montanari, *L'aziende curtense in Italia* (Bologna, 1985).

[23] Robert Fossier, 'Les tendances de l'économie: stagnation ou croissance?', in *Nascita dell'Europa ed Europa Carolingia* (Spoleto, 1981: Settimane di Studio del Centro italiano di studi sull'alto medioevo 27), pp. 261–74.

the presidency of Georges Duby, who himself in his book *Warriors and Peasants* in 1973 had made a similar judgement but who at Flaran did not commit himself. The major contribution to the Flaran meeting, which actually had as its central theme agricultural growth in the early Middle Ages, was that of Pierre Toubert on the role of the big manor in the 'take off' of the western economy during the eighth, ninth and tenth centuries. It is still the best analysis of the 'minimalist' views on Carolingian economy and at the same time a thorough refutation of them, based on recent scholarship and on primary sources alike.[24]

In the eyes of the minimalists the very low rentability of the big estate was one of the essential characteristics of the manorial production system. This statement was in the first place supported by demographic conjectures about the low population density of most regions, except where one cannot escape documentary evidence of the reverse, as in the Paris basin. Their interpretation of the vast average dimension of the *mansus* was also used as a demographic argument, again with the exception of the Paris basin. Low yield ratios and the reservation of a large part of the production for seed for the next year, for the army and for the supply of the king's or the lord's court, did not leave big grain surpluses for the market. 'Autoconsumption' was the rule and there was no incentive for reinvestment. Agricultural technique was primitive and agricultural instruments were scarce and made of wood. This kind of statement, mostly made without the thorough support of texts or other evidence, will be refuted in Chapter 3, drawing on Toubert's masterly contribution to the Flaran debate.

After this long concern with Carolingian agriculture and manorial organisation, a subject somewhat neglected by Pirenne, scholarship in the 1980s – after a twenty-year gap – reverted, in a third phase of post-Pirenne historiography, to Pirenne's favoured subject of trade and towns, now however from a totally new point of view hardly known during Pirenne's lifetime and mostly ignored by him: archaeology. Since the Second World War medieval archaeology had been emancipated from classical archaeology and was practised by archaeologists

---

[24] Pierre Toubert, 'La part du grand domaine dans le décollage économique de l'Occident (viiie–xe siècles)', in *La croissance agricole du Haut Moyen Âge* (Auch 1990: Flaran 10), pp. 53–86.

who were at the same time historians or at least had this ambition.[25] Among them Richard Hodges is the most engaged in the economic and social history of the Carolingian period, more particularly in the problems initiated by Pirenne. Like Toubert and most specialists of the matter today, Hodges considers the age of Charlemagne a period of economic growth, about which he has written several controversial books.[26] One important aspect of this controversy is his strong belief in the Carolingian origin of towns, more particularly those towns that around the middle of the ninth century succeeded as *portus* to the so-called *emporia*. Both types, in his opinion, contain the seed of urban development in the eleventh and twelfth centuries. This statement is more questionable concerning the *emporia* than with respect to the new *portus* of the ninth century. As contrasted with the former, most *portus* survived the Viking invasions without any significant break and gave birth, from the tenth century onwards, to important towns engaging in long-distance trade in the eleventh century. The *emporia* within the Carolingian empire, Dorestad, Quentovic and other minor ones (Medemblik, *Witla*), in contrast to places outside the empire, like London, Hamwic (Southampton) or Ribe, did not form the nucleus of a later town of some importance. This is our only point of discussion with Richard Hodges's recent views as exposed in his book *Towns and Trade in the Age of Charlemagne*.[27]

Thus the recent new interest in towns, especially from the side of archaeologists like Hodges, Hill, Van Es and others, will surely reopen the debate on *Mahomet et Charlemagne*, which is still not closed and will perhaps never be.

For my part I hope that some ideas put forward in this book will prove a valuable contribution to it.

---

[25] Herbert Jankuhn, Walter Schlesinger and Heiko Steuer (eds.), *Vor- und Frühformen der europäischen Stadt im Mittelalter*, 2 vols. (Göttingen, 1975: Abhandlungen der Akademie der Wissenschaften); Richard Hodges and Brian Hobley (eds.), *The Rebirth of Towns in the West AD 700–1050* (London, 1988: CBA Research Report 68); *La genèse et les premiers siècles des villes médiévales dans les Pays-Bas méridionaux. Un problème archéologique et historique* (Brussels 1990: Crédit Communal, coll. Histoire in-8°, no. 83); Clarke and Ambrosiani, *Towns in the Viking Age.*

[26] Richard Hodges, *Dark Age Economics. The Origins of Towns and Trade AD 600–1000* (London, 1982); Richard Hodges and David Whitehouse, *Mohammed, Charlemagne and the Origins of Europe* (London, 1983).

[27] Richard Hodges, *Towns and Trade in the Age of Charlemagne* (London: Duckworth, 2000).

PART I

LAND AND PEOPLE

I

LANDSCAPE AND SETTLEMENT

WOODLAND

The Carolingian landscape was for a large part, on the average for more than 40 per cent and in some regions up to 80 per cent, a natural landscape, consisting mainly of woods. The map of European forests in the early Middle Ages, made up by Charles Higounet, is still the best guide to study their geographical distribution.[1] He has localised and identified nearly 150 individual forests, some of which can be studied more in detail. Most of them lay east of the Rhine and along it, and also in the adjoining eastern parts of France and Belgium, a situation that lasted to the end of the Middle Ages and persists still today. In around 1500, one-third of Germany and a quarter of France were still covered by woodland. The larger part of these forests was royal land, protected by the king as hunting reserves, which is the original meaning of 'forest' (Lat. *forestis, forestum*). Some of these forests consisted not only of woods but included also uncultivated land, pasture, heath, moor and even arable land. In central Europe the Thuringian forest, in the middle of which the abbey of Fulda was founded in 742, may have been inhabited around that centre before the arrival of the monks. Clearances, named *capturae*, took place all around from the beginning of the eighth century and continued well into the ninth, perhaps related to the military operations of Charlemagne against

---

[1] Charles Higounet, 'Les forêts de l'Europe occidentale du ve au xie siècle', in *Agricoltura e mondo rurale in Occidente nell'alto medioevo* (Spoleto, 1966: Settimane di studio del Centro italiano di studi sull'alto medioevo 13), pp. 343–98.

the neighbouring Saxons.[2] A chain of forests along the right bank
of the Rhine, west of Thuringia and farther south, stretched from
the Westerwald and the Taunus in the north to the Odenwald in the
south. The latter was all royal land until it was ceded away to the
abbeys and churches of Fulda, Amorbach, Worms and particularly
Lorsch, which started an attack on the forest in 772. Only two
estates with arable land were organised within the Odenwald, the
most important of which was Michelstadt. Charlemagne's biographer
Einhard, who had received it from the emperor some years before,
gave it to Lorsch in 819 with a hundred unfree peasants. Other evidence of clearances or exploitation of the forest is lacking because the
geographical traces of internal colonisation, which Nitz dates in the
ninth century, should be placed in the tenth and eleventh centuries as
proposed by Chris Wickham.[3] Newly reclaimed land (called *bifangum*
and *proprisum*) was only mentioned at the edge of the Odenwald, at
Bensheim, between 765 and 850.

Left of the Rhine, massive forests on the Eifel plateau reached
Bonn and Aachen, to the west of which the Ardennes, as we know
them still today, were in Roman times and in the early Middle Ages
part of a far greater forest of that name. Near its centre, not far from
the abbey of Stavelot-Malmedy, the term *forestis* appears for the first
time in 648. Somewhat later several *forestes* are situated in the same
region, the north-east of the Ardennes and the least fertile part of
it, close to Aachen. This was the heartland of the Carolingians, a
vast royal domain with Roman roads between Cologne, Trier and
Reims across it and not unpopulated. No less than 25 exploitation
centres (*curtes, fisci*) were situated within it. New settlements from
the eighth century like the village of Villance near Bastogne, belonging to the abbey of Prüm, threatened the use-rights of the *fiscus* of
Theux and of the abbey of Stavelot-Malmedy.[4] More to the west in

[2] Chris Wickham, 'European Forests in the Early Middle Ages: Landscape and
Land Clearance', in Wickham, *Land and Power*, pp. 156–61; Dietrich Lohrmann,
'La croissance agricole en Allemagne au Haut Moyen Âge', in *La croissance agricole*
(= Flaran 10), pp. 109–13.

[3] Wickham, 'European Forests', pp. 179–83.

[4] René Noël, 'Pour une archéologie de la nature dans le nord de la "Francia" ', in
L'ambiente vegetale nell'alto medioevo (Spoleto, 1990: Settimane di studio del Centro
italiano di studi sull'alto medioevo 37), pp. 763–820; René Noël, 'Moines et nature
sauvage: dans l'Ardenne du haut moyen âge', in Jean-Marie Duvosquel and Alain
Dierkens (eds.), *Villes et campagnes au Moyen Âge. Mélanges Georges Despy* (Liège,
1991), pp. 563–97; Wickham, 'European Forests', pp. 175–9.

present-day Belgium, from the Scheldt near Tournai to the river Dyle near Leuven, several woods were the remnants of the former fifth- and sixth-century *sylva Carbonaria*, which had not been protected as a *forestis*. The 'forêt de Soignes', still existing today south-east of Brussels, is one of them. On less sandy soils in northern Flanders a forest called *Koningsforeest* in the twelfth century, refers by its name to its royal status in Carolingian times and to the protection that saved it from destruction. The same cannot be said of the *Sceldeholt*, a large wood south of Ghent, between the rivers Leie and Scheldt down to Kortrijk, which already in the ninth century belonged to the abbey of St Peter's at Ghent. By lack of protection it degenerated into heathland on the sandy soils of its northern half in the tenth and eleventh centuries because of the use-rights of the villagers living on the banks of both rivers.[5]

In France north of the Loire the largest forests, like the Der (*saltus Dervensis*), lay in the north-east. Here the abbey of Montiérender had its tenants undertake clearances, as we learn at length from the abbey's polyptych dating from shortly before 845.[6] The Paris region had some woods on the plateaux, like the Yvelines forest south-west of the city and the Brie east of it, but the whole region, especially the valleys, was densely populated.[7] To the west of Paris the abbey of St Germain-des-Prés around 825–9 had several wooded estates in the Perche region.[8] In these western parts of France the woods were rather fragmented and in the Loire region less densely wooded birch forests grew on the plateaux of the Sologne and the Gâtinais. South of the Loire only the Massif Central (Auvergne) and the region immediately north of the Garonne were densely wooded, but partly with degraded forests. Here indeed begin the 'fragile' woods of the Mediterranean type characterised by very difficult natural regeneration.

In Italy there was less and less dense woodland, except in some regions like the northern fringes of the plain of the river Po, the Ligurian and Tuscan Appenines, the Abruzzes and the pine woods

[5] Adriaan Verhulst, *Histoire du paysage rural en Flandre* (Brussels, 1966), pp. 87–98.

[6] Droste, *Polyptichon von Montierender*, v° *exarti*.

[7] Omer Tulippe, *L'habitat rural en Seine-et-Oise. Essai de géographie du peuplement* (Paris, Liège, 1934); M. Roblin, *Le terroir de Paris aux époques gallo-romaine et franque*, second edition (Paris, 1971).

[8] Konrad Elmshäuser and Andreas Hedwig, *Studien zum Polyptychon von Saint-Germain-des-Prés* (Cologne, Weimar, Vienna, 1993), pp. 130–5, 405.

in Calabria. In the Sabina Chris Wickham studied more than twenty *gualdi*, a particular type of fiscal land consisting not only of wood (*gualdus* = Germ. *Wald*) but also of other uncultivated land, pasture and even arable, cultivated by *coloni publici*, free men owing dues to the duke of Spoleto but degraded to tenants of the abbey of Farfa after many *gualdi* had been given or sold to the latter. These *gualdi* may be compared to the *Bifänge* and *capturae* in Germany and the status of their inhabitants to that of the *aprisionarii* who repopulated the Languedoc and Catalonia in the ninth century after their desertion as the consequence of Arab invasions.

Entities like the *gualdi* are an example of the mixed woodland–arable economy that characterised large parts of Carolingian Europe, where there was no opposition between nature and culture 'for woodland was widely exploited in all periods; nor should one oppose woodland exploitation and arable cultivation, for both formed a normal part of peasant subsistence strategies and landlordly expropriation alike'.[9]

FIELDS AND VILLAGES

The configuration of woods in Carolingian Europe, as it has been described, does not allow us simply to fill in the open spaces between them with regions where arable land is supposed to have been dominant. There were, however, such regions in the eighth and ninth centuries and it makes sense indeed to analyse the structure of their settlements and fields, as far as they have been the object of detailed study, although one must be careful with generalisations. The Paris region, on the basis of the early-ninth-century polyptych of St Germain-des-Prés, can be such a test case and also the Ghent region in Flanders by using the book of gifts (*Liber traditionum*) made in the eighth and ninth centuries to the abbey of St Peter's in Ghent. They were among the most densely populated regions of north-west Europe, the distribution of rural settlements of which may be illustrated, to begin with, by the example of the Germanic speaking regions of Belgium in the early Middle Ages.[10]

---

[9] Wickham, 'European Forests', pp. 162–70, 198.
[10] Adriaan Verhulst, 'Settlement and Field Structures in Continental North-West Europe from the Ninth to the Thirteenth Centuries', *Medieval Settlement Research Group. Annual Report* 13 (1998), pp. 6–13.

From the fifth well into the ninth century this distribution was characterised by a majority of dispersed settlements, mainly consisting of mostly newly created hamlets and isolated farmsteads. The evidence for this are the numerous names ending in *-inga haim*, *-haim*, *-sali* and even *-thorp*, that occur in written documents of the eighth, ninth and tenth centuries. In later centuries, however, many (if not the majority of them) cannot be identified with the name of a village, a hamlet or even a farmstead. In the rare cases where we still find them in a document of the twelfth or thirteenth century, they are often mere field names. Of the four types cited, the names ending in *-sali* most clearly denote an isolated farmstead. This interpretation results from their meaning – a house in which the livestock are sheltered under the same roof as the family – from their location and function – they are very often situated in woodland and devoted to the breeding of cattle and sheep as is apparent in both cases from the word composed with *-sali* – and finally they are described in Latin texts as *mansioniles*, a term pointing to their status as a dependency of a manor, smaller and created at a later date. Linguistically, too, they are later than the names ending in *-inga haim*, as is also the case with the names ending in *-haim*. In Romanic-speaking regions the *-villare* settlements may be compared to the *-sali* farmsteads both on linguistic grounds – *villare* being a diminutive of *villa* – and on the basis of manorial texts suggesting their dependence on a *villa*. The evidence about the names ending in *-sali*, and possibly this holds good for the names ending in *-haim* too, gives support to the supposition that from the seventh to the ninth century the dispersion of rural settlement increased. This does not necessarily mean that during the same period hamlets did not grow into larger groupings of farmsteads to which the term 'village' might be applied, probably and still for a certain time without its juridical connotation, which is a phenomenon of the eleventh and twelfth centuries. Schwind[11] has shown the existence among the landed possessions of the abbey of Lorsch in the middle Rhine region during the ninth century of at least two fairly big groupings of thirty to thirty-five farmsteads that he does not hesitate to call villages in the geographical sense. They were indeed, as Schwind could prove from inventories and charters, nucleated villages, in which the farmsteads lay side by side. Consequently their

---

[11] Fred Schwind, 'Beobachtungen zur inneren Struktur des Dorfes in karolingischer Zeit', in Jankuhn, Schutzeichel and Schwind (eds.), *Dorf der Eisenzeit*, pp. 444–93.

lands must have been located outside the village, perhaps in an open-
field layout as is still the case today. It is not clear to what extent
the structuring of a manor by the abbey, which is apparent from the
organisation into fiscal units (*hubae, mansi*) of the lands acquired by
gifts, fostered this grouping. Neither do we know if this structuring led to the abandonment of isolated settlements. The field layout
of the early Middle Ages and the formation of the open field can
perhaps throw more light upon such problems.

   Before studying these aspects of the early medieval cultural landscape, the settlements in the Paris region should be examined, especially those that in Carolingian times were the centre of manors
of St Germain-des-Prés at a small distance south and south-east of
Paris.[12] Contrasting with the above described settlements in Flanders,
they were all of Gallo-Roman origin. Their Roman antecedents were
settlement cells that were starting points for the organisation, mostly
by the Merovingian king whose property they were, of manors which
took the Gallo-Roman name of the settlement. They were located
along watercourses not far from Roman roads and expanded, through
clearances that ended some time before the creation of Irmino's
polyptych (825–9), from the valleys up to the rich loamy plateaux
where the main blocks of arable were situated. These plateaux had
been covered with woods and heath as is suggested by many placenames. The clearances had probably been due to the initiative of the
abbey after it had received the estate by royal gift, whilst the foun-
dation of a church in the settlement centre had in some cases been
done by the king. The oldest were dedicated to St Martin and St Peter
and may have been founded by the Merovingian king, whereas the
younger had St Germain as patron and were clearly founded by the
abbey.

   The church was the centre of the settlement as was proved by excavations in a few *villae* of the abbey of St Denis in the same Paris
region.[13] In Villers-le-Sec three clusters of buildings, which have
been interpreted as three *mansi*, lay around the cemetery and a small
open place near the church, at the crosspoint of two roads. The
mansi were separated by small roads or paths at distances of 80, 70
and 30 metres from each other. This is the prefiguration of a village

[12] Elmshäuser and Hedwig, *Studien zum Polyptychon Saint-Germain-des-Prés*,
     pp. 35–6, 77–9.
[13] Jean Cuisenier and Rémy Guadagnin (eds.), *Un village au temps de Charlemagne*
     (Paris, 1988), pp. 118–21, 142–9.

structure, not yet very concentrated as will be the result of its evolution in the tenth to eleventh centuries. The buildings of the *mansi*
consisted of a living house 12.5 metres long in which cattle were sheltered, and a few other buildings, amongst which were some 'sunken
huts' occupying very unequal plots, from 40 ares to 18 hectares.

The arable lands of these farms must very probably be sought outside the village proper but very little is known about them. We may,
however, be sure that the peasants' lands did not lie intermingled with
the arable lands of the lord's central court, the *mansus indominicatus* of
the manor, for we are well informed on the demesne by the polyptych of abbot Irmino of St Germain-des-Prés (*c*. 825–9), although
not on the material aspects of the *mansus indominicatus* of St Denis in
Villers-le-Sec, which has not been excavated.

The arable land of the demesnes of St Germain-des-Prés in the
neighbourhood of Paris consisted of fields called *culturae*.[14] There
were large and smaller ones and each *villa* had between four and
twelve of them. The small *culturae* measured from 5 to 16 hectares,
whereas the larger ones extended over 66 to 88 hectares. They formed
different entities of demesne land, often enclosed by non-temporary
hedges and well marked off from the peasants' lands. Within them
temporary wooden fences were often placed by the services of the
tenants to protect the parts that were sown with grain, when part
of the *cultura* lay fallow and was used as pasture. It is plausible to consider this as a prefiguration of the later fully developed three-course
field system rather than to interpret, as some historians have done,
the *culturae* in their totality as furlongs in such a system. This difficult
question will be explained in Chapter 4. From the geographical point
of view, which is mainly ours for the moment, it is sufficient to say
that these *culturae*, each in itself formed an 'open field' or rather what
has been called a 'micro-open field', without the whole region having an open aspect and certainly without considering the Carolingian
field system as the 'open-field system' proper of later centuries.

A very different picture of the Carolingian agricultural landscape
emerges from the analysis of the gifts recorded in the *Liber Traditionum*
of St Peter's abbey in Ghent.[15] A large number of gifts from the ninth
century to this abbey are concentrated in the territory of the village of

[14] Elmshäuser and Hedwig, *Studien*, pp. 348–53.
[15] Adriaan Verhulst, 'Le paysage rural en Flandre intérieure: son évolution entre le
IXe et le XIIIe siècle', *Revue du Nord* 62 (1980), pp. 11–30, reprinted in Verhulst,
Rural and Urban Aspects, VIII.

Sint-Martens-Latem, situated on the banks of the river Leie some
10 kilometres south of Ghent. These gifts consist of modest to very
small peasant holdings of between 2.5 and 5 hectares, the lands of
which are scattered over four to five fields, each bearing a name composed with the suffix -*accra*: *Hostaraccara* (var. *Ostar*), *Euinaccar, Hanria
accara, Brainna accara, Helsaccra*. Only the last of these field names can
be identified with a later and still existing one (Elsakker), situated
near two other *akker*-names of younger date, but all three signifi-
cantly lying beside the main arable field of the village which in texts
from the later Middle Ages is called *Latemkouter*, a name composed
of the name of the village and the Flemish word *kouter*. I will come
to the latter in a moment. Before that it is important to note that in
the Ghent region the same configuration occurs regularly, although
in texts from the later Middle Ages: names ending in -*akker* for small
fields beside a big field called *kouter,* the latter bearing the name of
the village or in several cases the name of a hamlet. While these
still existing *kouter*-names cannot be found in our early medieval
texts, the latter do preserve many more names composed with *accra*
(*accarom, accarum, accrum, agrum*), all from the ninth century and all
situated not too far (up to 25 kilometres) from Ghent. Like those
from Sint-Martens-Latem cited above they are difficult to localise
or to identify with a later field name. This time however, in contrast with the names ending in -*accra* cited above, the first element
of most names is the name of a kin settlement: -*inga*; or of a larger
settlement interpreting the element *inga*: -*inga haim*; for example
Ramaringahemia agrum, Culingahem accra, Eninga accra. Consequently
they may be interpreted as the name of the principal field of the
settlement. Besides this field these settlements had other fields, some
with a name ending in -*accra* composed with a point of the compass
(*Westeraccra, Sudaccra*), the name of a person (*Euinaccar*) or otherwise
(*Stenaccra*), some with a name pointing to the origin of the field as
newly cleared land (*Heninga rodha* at *Eninga, Rodha* at *Culingahem*),
some indicating uncleared land (*Ramaringahemia mariscum*).

   Because the names of these settlements and their fields have nearly
all disappeared in later centuries, it is very difficult to make an appeal
to later sources and landscapes in order to interpret the early medieval
evidence. More particularly we cannot say much about the devel-
opments between the ninth and the thirteenth century and hence
explain the disappearance of most of these names. It is nevertheless
striking that in the later Middle Ages, especially in the Ghent region

but also more generally in the south of east Flanders, in the valleys of the rivers Scheldt and Leie and not far from the language boundary, the majority of the villages, and even smaller hamlets on the territory of the same village, have a principal field bearing the name of the village or the hamlet followed by the suffix *-kouter*. As I have already said, most of the *-akker* names had disappeared by that time, except some that were not formed from a settlement name and which were situated at the edge of the main *kouter*. It therefore looks as if the ninth-century *-accra* names composed with a settlement name have been replaced between the ninth and the thirteenth century by *-kouter* names, but to explain this would mean going beyond the Carolingian period.

The evidence obtained so far from written sources concerning early medieval field structures has shown that *culturae*, *akkers* and *kouters* in north-west Europe generally consisted of large blocks of arable land, seldom subdivided into smaller plots. This observation is confirmed, either by written documents or by archaeological evidence for regions as far away as Auvergne or the Bas-Languedoc.[16] In the southern half of France a link has been observed between the early medieval blocks and protohistoric fields and more frequently with a Roman *centuriatio*.[17] A similar link has been suggested with the so-called 'Celtic' fields in north-west Europe[18] and even with *centuriatio*-like structures in north-eastern Belgium[19] and central and

---

[16] Gabriel Fournier, *Le peuplement rural en Basse Auvergne durant le haut moyen âge* (Paris, 1962), pp. 322–5; Monique Bourin, 'Délimitation des parcelles et perception de l'espace en Bas-Languedoc aux xe et xie siècles', in *Campagnes médiévales: l'homme et son espace. Etudes offertes à Robert Fossier* (Paris, 1995), p. 79.

[17] Gérard Chouquer, 'Parcellaires et longue durée', in Gérard Chouquer (ed.), *Les formes du paysage*, 3 vols. (Paris, 1996), vol. II, *Archéologie des parcellaires*, pp. 213–18; Jean-Loup Abbé, 'Permanences et mutations des parcellaires médiévaux', *ibid.*, pp. 223–33.

[18] This opinion of the Dutch archaeologist H. T. Waterbolk, 'Patterns of the Peasant Landscape', *Proceedings of the Prehistoric Society* 61 (1995), pp. 1–36, concerning the continuity of landscape and settlement from prehistoric to historic times in the Dutch province of Drenthe, is no longer accepted: Theo Spek, 'Die bodenkundliche und landschaftliche Lage von Siedlungen, Äkkern und Gräberfeldern in Drenthe (nördliche Niederlande)', *Siedlungsforschung* 14 (1996), pp. 95–193, esp. 142–56 (with an English summary).

[19] Joseph R. Mertens, 'Sporen van Romeins kadaster in Limburg?', *Limburg* 37 (1958), pp. 1–7, reprinted in *Acta Archaeologica Lovaniensia* 25 (1986), xx; Ludo Melard, 'Millen. Van natuurlandschap tot cultuurlandschap', *Volkskunde* 87(1986), pp. 262–345, esp. pp. 282–90.

northern France,[20] which are, however, difficult to establish as such, let alone as precursors of early medieval field forms.

The blocks composing the *culturae* of northern France and southern Belgium belonged as a whole to one owner, the lord of the manor, as part of the so-called 'réserve' (demesne) in a classical bipartite estate. The same is not always sure for the ninth-century fields with a settlement name followed by the suffix *-accra* in the Ghent region and in south-east Flanders.[21] Only when in their totality they were integrated into a manorial structure was this the case, as some examples in and near Ghent demonstrate at a later time when the *-accra* names had already disappeared and been replaced by *-kouter* names. Elsewhere on large fields named after the settlement followed by the suffix *-accra*, peasant plots must have been lying intermingled with lands of the lord who represented the kin or family that had given its name ending in *-inga* to the settlement. The lands of the lord can in later centuries and on early modern cadastral plans be identified as large blocks of irregular form whereas the peasant plots generally formed small strips brought together in furlongs laid out in the same direction.

These patterns and more particularly the division of block parcels or furlongs into strips can seldom be observed from contemporary early medieval written evidence. The polyptych of abbot Irmino (825–9) however gives some information on the size of plots belonging to the *ancinga*, that is that part of the demesne divided up among the tenants and which they had to cultivate the whole year round for their lord. These plots were long narrow strips whose length was eight, ten to twenty-five times their width.[22] Some rare texts from the tenth and eleventh centuries, giving the length or width (or both) of plots or indications of their boundaries or of their neighbouring plots, have been studied in the Auvergne and Languedoc by French historians.[23] Their conclusions converge in so far as an evolution away

[20] A. Querrien, 'Parcellaires antiques et médiévaux du Berry', *Journal des Savants* (1994), pp. 235–366, esp. pp. 307–10; R. Agache, *La Somme pré-romaine et romaine* (Amiens, 1978: Mémoires de la Société des Antiquaires de Picardie, in-4° series, 24), pp. 454–6.

[21] Verhulst, 'Paysage rural en Flandre intérieure'.

[22] Elmshäuser and Hedwig, *Studien*, p. 356.

[23] Gabriel Fournier, *Le peuplement rural en Basse-Auvergne durant le haut moyen âge* (Paris, 1962); Bourin, 'Délimitation des parcelles'; A. Guerreau, 'L'évolution du parcellaire en Mâconnais (env.900–env.1060)', in L. Feller, P. Mane and F. Piponnier (eds.), *Le village médiéval et son environnement. Etudes offertes à Jean-Marie Pesez* (Paris, 1998), pp. 509–35.

from block fields to smaller and sometimes more irregular parcels can be observed in the tenth to eleventh centuries. Only on newly cleared land regular strips represent from the eleventh century onwards the dominant field structure of the later Middle Ages.

TOWNS

Towns, although occupying a relatively small part of the soil and not very numerous in Carolingian times, are an element of the not very urbanised cultural landscape of that period and should therefore be considered here. Their geographical aspects, only briefly touched on in Chapter 7, will be dealt with here, with an emphasis on those towns of Roman origin that were still the majority in the Carolingian empire, with the exception of the regions east of the Rhine. The new towns, the so-called *emporia*, have been treated at length in their geographical aspects as part of the infrastructure of Carolingian trade in Chapter 7.

At the end of the third century, Roman towns had shrunk as new stone walls were built around them and suburbs, artisanal quarters and other peripheral elements were left outside the walls. Not only here but also inside the new walls a certain ruralisation took place. Open spaces became larger and more numerous. Public buildings decayed, became part of the defensive construct and were sometimes occupied by private persons, subdivided and used as private dwellings. This process went on until the seventh century when churches and newly founded abbeys were built on the ruins of Roman buildings and with stones from them, on the same spot or farther away in the suburban zone. The old Roman wall lost its significance, fell in ruins and the transition between town and countryside became vaguer. As another consequence of these changes the centre of the town often shifted away from its former place.[24]

At the end of the eighth century intense building activity around the cathedrals in many episcopal cities like Metz, Lyon, Vienne, Le Mans and others, was provoked by the new regulations about the life in common of the canons, prescribed in 754 by Chrodegang, bishop of Metz, and imposed throughout his kingdom by Charlemagne.

---

[24] N. Christie and S. T. Loseby (eds.), *Towns in Transition: Urban Evolution in Late Antiquity and the Early Middle Ages* (Aldershot, 1996); Terry R. Slater (ed.), *Towns in Decline AD 100–1600* (Aldershot, 2000).

Ruralisation of the urban landscape clearly came to a halt but no
new walls were built.[25]

The old Roman walls of some *civitates* like Tournai were restored
in the second half of the ninth century against possible attacks by
the Vikings. Often abbeys like St Denis, St Vaast in Arras, St Bavo
in Ghent, which like many others (Lorsch, St Riquier, Fulda) had
meanwhile been rebuilt in the new Carolingian style, were walled for
the same reason.[26] Near them and included in their later fortification,
monastic cities developed from the late eighth century onwards in
Tours, St Riquier (*Centula*), Arras, Ghent and elsewhere.[27] Being at
the service of the abbey they were not autonomous but nevertheless,
at least geographically, had an urban character, with houses, workshops and shops along streets. Some, like the monastic city called
portus near St Bavo's abbey in Ghent (around 865), played an economic role in the outside world and were inhabited by merchants
who, besides their activity at the service of the abbey, may have set
up an independent trade for their own profit.

---

[25] Jean Hubert, 'La renaissance carolingienne et la topographie religieuse des cités
épiscopales', in *I problemi della civiltà carolingia* (Spoleto, 1954: Settimane di
studio del Centro italiano di studi sull'alto medioevo, 1), pp. 219–25; Werner
Jacobsen, 'Die Renaissance der frühchristlichen Architektur in der Karolingerzeit',
in Christoph Stiegemann and Matthias Wemhoff (eds.), *Kunst und Kultur der
Karolingerzeit* (Mainz, 1999), pp. 623–43.
[26] Adriaan Verhulst, *The Rise of Cities in North-West Europe* (Cambridge, 1999),
pp. 59–67.
[27] Fred Schwind, 'Zu karolingerzeitlichen Klöstern als Wirtschaftsorganismen
und Stätten handwerklicher Produktion', in L. Fenske, W. Rösener and Th.
Zotz (eds.), *Institutionen, Kultur und Gesellschaft im Mittelalter. Festschrift für Josef
Fleckenstein* (Sigmaringen, 1984), pp. 101–23.

2

DEMOGRAPHY

———— • ————

Conjectures about the demographic situation and evolution in Carolingian Europe have been based mainly on four polyptychs containing demographically usable data such as names, figures, family structure and even age of tenants, inhabitants and dependants of manors. They are, in order of importance of the information, the polyptych of the abbey of St Germain-des-Prés under abbot Irmino (825–9), of the abbey of St Bertin (844–59), of St Remi de Reims under archbishop Hincmar (middle ninth century) and of St Victor de Marseilles (813–14).[1] Their value in this respect has been much criticised, most severely by Léon-R. Ménager,[2] but the studies by Jean-Pierre Devroey of certain aspects of their redaction[3] have cleared

[1] Hägermann, *Polyptychon Saint-Germain-des-Prés*; Ganshof, *Polyptyque Saint-Bertin*; Devroey, *Polyptyque Saint-Remi de Reims*; Benjamin Guérard, Léopold Delisle and A. Marion, *Cartulaire de l'abbaye de Saint-Victor de Marseille* (Paris, 1857), no. 31.

[2] Léon-R. Ménager, 'Considérations sociologiques sur la démographie des grands domaines ecclésiastiques carolingiens', in *Etudes d'histoire du droit canonique dédiées à Gabriel Le Bras*, 2 vols. (Paris, 1965), vol. II, pp. 1317–35.

[3] Jean-Pierre Devroey, 'A propos d'un article récent: l'utilisation du polyptyque d'Irminon en démographie', *Revue belge de philologie et d'histoire* 55(1977), pp. 509–14; Jean-Pierre Devroey, 'Les méthodes d'analyse démographique des polyptyques du haut moyen âge', *Acta Historica Bruxellensia* 4(1981), pp. 71–88, both reprinted in Jean-Pierre Devroey, *Etudes sur le grand domaine carolingien* (Aldershot 1993: Variorum), nos. IV and V.

the way for a synthesis by Pierre Toubert which has met a large consensus.[4]

Being static documents polyptychs give a snapshot picture of some demographic aspects of a manor, some of which, however, are elements of a dynamic mechanism. This is, for example, the case of the ratio of adults to children, especially female adults, from which conjectures about future growth or stagnation of the population can be made. Using such data one must look out for possible and in fact frequent over- or under-representation of some categories of the population. Duby, for example, concluded erroneously that stagnation and even crisis characterised the demographic evolution of the manor of Villeneuve-Saint-Georges. He then, in combination with other factors, generalised this conclusion.[5] Devroey has since proved that the number of children and women in the polyptych of Irmino has been under-represented. An apparent over-representation of males, which had formerly been explained by male immigration, infanticide of females, etc., appeared to be the result of certain particularities in the make-up of polyptychs concerning immigrants.

Notwithstanding these difficulties and pitfalls, some general conclusions, as formulated by Toubert, have been widely accepted. The predominance of the 'simple' family, composed of the parents and the children, numbering 4.5 to 5.5 persons, is one of the most important. Three children per couple was an average. The old idea of the large 'patriarchal' family, with grandparents and unmarried brothers or sisters living under the same roof, has to be rejected. So-called 'over-populated' *mansi* were not exploited by patriarchal families or perhaps even joint families, although, as Bessmerny has maintained,[6] simple families were overarched in larger economic and familial groupings. On the manors of St Germain-des-Prés 30 to 60 per cent of the holdings were exploited by co-tenants, of which according to Bessmerny 20 to 25 per cent were related to the principal tenant and were mostly elder children of the latter. These co-tenants lived separately and consequently the number of *foci* (hearths) was much higher than

[4] Pierre Toubert, 'Le moment carolingien (VIIIe-Xe siècle)', in André Burguière, Christiane Klapisch-Zuber *et al.* (eds.), *Histoire de la famille*, 2 vols. (Paris, 1986), vol. I, pp. 333–59.
[5] Georges Duby, *The Early Growth of the European Economy. Warriors and Peasants from the Seventh to the Twelfth Century* (Ithaca, 1978), pp. 81–2.
[6] J. Bessmerny, 'Les structures de la famille paysanne dans les villages de la Francia au IXe siècle', *Le Moyen Age* 90 (1984), pp. 165–93.

the number of *mansi*. How exactly the *mansus* was exploited in such cases is not clear. In the end it was divided but that division may not be seen as a sign of crisis but as the expression of the fact that the *mansus*-system was no longer adapted to the demographic situation. Toubert considers this division to be the result of a dynamic policy from above, favouring small exploitations that maximised the rentability of smaller demesnes through a more disposable labour force.

The polyptych of St Victor de Marseilles, by recording the age of children, enables something to be said about the evolution of population figures at the beginning of the ninth century, at least in Provence.[7] The numerical differences in the age groups of young children, the youngest being less numerous than the preceding group, suggests the existence of cyclical crises at short intervals in 803–6 and 810–14, possibly corresponding to famines in 803, 805 and 807 and to a cattle-plague sparking over to men in 810. The presence of a large group of youngsters may be an answer to earlier crises. These crises may however have been very local, but the quick fluctuations point in any case to a fragile demographic situation, sensitive to sudden crises but capable of filling up the gaps rapidly. The number of children per couple, 2.9 to 3.1 in Provence, was a good basis for future growth. Fertility coefficients derived from the proportion of adults to children make it possible to assume that the population of certain estates in the eighth and ninth centuries doubled in a time span of half to one and a half centuries. A doubling in 100 years, that is a growth of 1 per cent a year, is accepted by several authors and probably occurred from as early as the seventh century.

There is less agreement on the answer to whether Carolingian population growth, which can be considered moderate to considerable, was a continuous process or whether it was interrupted by times of crisis. Many authors refer in this respect to the numerous famines which struck the central areas of the Carolingian empire in the northern half of France at the end of the eighth and the beginning of the ninth century. These famines were so severe that they forced Charlemagne to take general and drastic measures in 794 such as setting maximum prices for bread and grain, introducing new units of measurement, weight and currency, establishing help

---

[7] Monique Zerner-Chardavoine, 'Enfants et jeunes au ixe siècle. La démographie du polyptyque de Marseille 813–814', *Provence Historique* 31 (1988), pp. 355–77. Opposite views by Stephen Weinberger, 'Peasant Households in Provence: ca 800–1100', *Speculum* 48 (1973), pp. 247–57.

for the needy and requiring the saying of prayers in churches and monasteries.[8] Usually, however, these famines are interpreted as accidents of growth, as expressions of a disproportion between a rapidly growing population and a rigid economic structure, especially on the large estates, where the so-called overpopulation of the *mansus* is in this respect referred to, both in the Île de France and in parts of northern Italy.[9] It is, however, not established that these consecutive famines had cumulative effects as was the case in the fourteenth and fifteenth centuries. There may have been rapid recovery after a famine, which in turn could have been the result of the dynamic qualities of a young population. A sensitivity to crises, more particularly to grain crises and the rapid and dynamic reactions afterwards, may be responsible for the apparently somewhat chaotic and uneven growth. Such a characteristic of early medieval demographic evolution is probably partly responsible for the fact that these fluctuations cannot be determined or delimited chronologically. Although growth of the population is a generally accepted fact for the whole of the Carolingian world all the evidence for it, however, is indirect.

For example, archaeological investigation of burial fields is only possible for the Merovingian period because christianisation from the seventh to the ninth century led to the burying of the dead in cemeteries near the church. Near Cologne in Germany a comparison between a sixth- and a seventh-century burial field points to an increase in population in that part of the Rhineland of up to 60 per cent in 100 years. This is not particularly high, and in Alemannia an extraordinary increase of three to six times the population of the sixth century was probably due to external causes such as immigrations.[10] In the Charente (south-west France) and the Mâconnais (southern Burgundy) the extension of burial fields in some villages has been interpreted as evidence for the doubling of their population between the beginning of the sixth and the middle of the seventh century.

Clearances are the most generally used indicator for population growth although their evidence may be very local and dangerous to generalise. Pollen analyses in various areas of Germany such as the Rhön and Eifel show a clear increase in grain pollen from the seventh century onwards. This points to the extension of arable land, which

---

[8] See Chapter 9.
[9] Toubert, 'La part du grand domaine', p. 64.
[10] Lohrmann, 'Croissance agricole', pp. 104–9.

is also borne out indirectly by some admittedly rare and isolated texts from the seventh century.

The earliest more explicit written records of land clearance concern the surroundings of Fulda in Thuringia during the second half of the eighth century. Particular mention is made of well-delimited virgin lands called *porprisum*, *bifang* or *captura* in which estates and farms were established by reclamation of new land.[11] There were twelve in the eighth century and thirty-six in the first thirty to forty years of the ninth century. These clearances were not primarily the work of the abbey but of laymen who subsequently donated the *bifang* to the abbey for further extension. Elsewhere in Germany, more particularly in south-west Germany and especially at the edges of the Odenwald, numerous reclamations in the form of *bifang* or *captura* are mentioned in the records of the abbeys of Lorsch and Fulda in the ninth century. Again they were, in a first phase, the work of laymen who can be characterised as entrepreneurs. Despite these examples being located mainly in Germany, the phenomenon was so widespread in western Europe, as has been illustrated in our overview of the distribution of forests, that it cannot reflect local coincidences.

In some regions of western Europe, however, the presence of large areas of arable land is probably responsible for the absence of written documents on new reclamations. Some of them, moreover, had, as early as the beginning of the ninth century, very high population densities. The area of Paris, the Île de France, is often mentioned as an example in this respect, partly because demographically useful data can be found in the famous polyptych of Abbot Irmino of the abbey of St Germain-des-Prés, which dates from shortly before 829.[12] On the basis of this document, population densities of thirty-nine inhabitants per square kilometre have been calculated for a number of abbey estates in the southern area of Paris, and appear to be indirectly confirmed by high densities of approximately thirty-four inhabitants per square kilometre on some estates of the abbey of St Bertin in the vicinity of St Omer in north-west France. However, concerning the latter, Schwarz has proposed a reduction to an average of twenty inhabitants per square kilometre.[13] A similar figure has been advanced

[11] Lohrmann, 'Croissance agricole', pp. 110–12.
[12] Monique Zerner, 'La population de Villeneuve-Saint-Georges et Nogent-sur-Marne au IXe siècle d'après le polyptyque de Saint-Germain-des-Prés', *Annales de la Faculté des Lettres et des Sciences Humaines de Nice* 37 (1979), pp. 17–24.
[13] G. M. Schwarz, 'Village Populations According to the Polyptyque of the Abbey of St Bertin', *Journal of Medieval History* 11(1985), pp. 31–41.

for the most densely populated area of Friesland (Westergo) around 900.[14] It is probably the case, however, that apart from these privileged areas (both demographically and as far as documents are concerned), the population density in many areas, even though they had been largely reclaimed, was much lower, and probably from four or five to between nine and twelve per square kilometre. There is general agreement on one thing in this respect: the population density and degree of arable land could vary largely from area to area and even from locality to locality, according to the age of occupation, the relative fertility and productivity of the soil, and types of land use. Compared with areas of southern Gaul and the Île de France in the north, to the Rhine/Moselle area, to the area between the Scheldt and the Dender in Belgium and others, there were thinly populated regions such as south-west and western France (Maine) or the northern half of Belgium.

[14] Bernard H. Slicher van Bath, 'The Economic and Social Conditions in the Frisian Districts from 900 to 1500', *AAG Bijdragen* 13 (1965), pp. 100–3.

PART II

PRODUCTION

3

AGRICULTURAL PRODUCTION

·

INTRODUCTION: THE GENERAL SETTING

Carolingian agriculture was, to an extent, practised by free independent peasants, though these had probably been more numerous in the preceding Merovingian period. The discussion in this chapter will concentrate on big landownership because so little is known about free independent peasants compared with what we know about large estates. The Carolingian state, particularly its military organisation, was in principle based upon the existence of a large class of free people, mainly peasants.[1] Gifts of landed property to churches, especially in the eighth and ninth centuries, were often made by free people who ran a peasant farm, sometimes with the help of unfree servants (*mancipia*). Nearly nothing is known about the size of these farms, which can be supposed to have been diverse. Peasants might have enjoyed rights in the woods, pastures and other uncultivated land belonging to the community whose members they were. The location and composition of this community is a problem, for its relation to the population centre of an organised big estate is not at all clear. Often, independent peasant farms were located near or even in the midst of royal or ecclesiastical manors.[2]

---

[1] Hans-Werner Goetz, 'Social and Military Institutions', in Rosamond McKitterick (ed.), *The New Cambridge Medieval History* (Cambridge, 1995), vol. II, pp. 458–60; Yoshiki Morimoto, 'Autour du grand domaine carolingien', pp. 64–5.

[2] Dopsch, *Wirtschaftsentwicklung*, I, pp. 138–40.

The most widely diffused form of agricultural activity, however, particularly in the Carolingian period, was that of dependent peasants, not totally free and even unfree, within what we call a manor (Lat. *villa*, or *fiscus* when in royal hands). Royal manors were particularly numerous around the rivers Aisne, Oise, Meuse, Moselle, Rhine and Main and more eastwards in Franconia, Thuringia and Bavaria.[3] Many functioned as residences of the itinerant king and were called *palatium*. The biggest *fisci* consisted of several often vast *villae* which in turn included smaller manors called *mansioniles*. Most famous is a group of *villae* and *mansioniles* around the central manor (*caput fisci*) Annappes near the town of Lille in France, close to the Belgian border. The sizes were 2,063 hectars for Annappes, with three *mansioniles* of 200 to 300 hectares and respectively 1,867, about 1,400 and 1,855 hectares for three *villae*.[4] The description and inventory of Annappes in a document *c.* 800, known as *Brevium exempla*, which will be commented upon below, begins as follows with the description and inventory of the buildings of the central manor:[5]

We found on the crown estate of Asnapium a royal house built of stone in the very best manner, having three rooms. The entire house was surrounded by galleries and it had eleven apartments for women. Underneath was one cellar. There were two porches. There were seventeen other houses built of wood within the court-yard, with a similar number of rooms and other amenities, all well constructed. There was one stable, one kitchen, one bakehouse, two barns, three haylofts. The yard was enclosed with a hedge and a stone gateway, with a gallery above from which distributions can be made. There was also an inner yard, surrounded by a hedge, well arranged and planted with various kinds of trees.

Bishop churches and abbeys, whose real property in the ninth century was equally important, had built up through gifts of kings, aristocrats and ordinary people, an immense patrimony mostly consisting of manors. The abbey of St Germain-des-Prés had 25 *villae* listed in the famous polyptych of abbot Irmino from *c.* 825–9, which was a minimum. Together they represented about 30,000 hectars of land and

---

[3] Metz, *Karolingische Reichsgut*.   4 Verhein, 'Studien Reichsgut', pp. 333–92.

[5] A. Boretius (ed.), *Capitularia regum Francorum*, 2 vols. (Hanover, 1883; reprint 1984), vol. I, no. 128; translation by Frederic A. Ogg (ed.), *A Sourcebook of Mediaeval History* (New York, 1907; reprint 1972), pp. 127–129, part of *Internet Medieval Sourcebook*, ed. P. Halsall, and by H. R. Loyn and John Percival, *The Reign of Charlemagne. Documents on Carolingian Government and Administration* (London, 1975), pp. 98–105.

woods. Smaller abbeys had ten to twenty *villae* with several hundreds of hectares of arable land each.

The real property of the aristocracy was generally less important, except that of some big families, related to the king, known as 'imperial aristocracy' (Germ. *Reichsaristokratie*). Estates of the aristocracy were, more than others, exposed to partitions through successions, gifts and the like, and many lay possessions consisted of what were called *portiones*. When churches had acquired them by gifts, these *portiones* were often brought together and reorganised as a manor.[6]

THE ORIGINS OF THE CLASSICAL BIPARTITE MANOR

From about the middle of the eighth century onwards, the structure and exploitation of big landownership in the Frankish empire between the Loire and the Rhine, between the Rhine, the Elbe and the Alps, and in northern and central Italy underwent profound changes. At different times, and in different ways, depending on the region and many other factors, the so-called bipartite structure was introduced on the big estates of the king, the church and the aristocracy.[7] In its most mature form the bipartite system consisted of an equilibrium between, and a close link in terms of exploitation with, the two parts that together constituted the unit of ownership referred to as a *villa*: one part, that is the demesne (Fr. *réserve*, Germ. *Salland*), was cultivated directly for the lord of the domain, mainly by the farmers among whom the other part of the estate was divided, the so-called tenements, tenures or holdings. The tenants could cultivate the latter for themselves in exchange for services, deliveries of goods and payments to the lord and his demesne. This mostly abstract model, the so-called classical form, occurred almost nowhere in its ideal form. And the model was not static, but constantly in evolution.

The general impression is that the bipartite system probably originated in the central parts of the Frankish realm, more particularly in

---

[6] Stéphane Lebecq, 'The Role of Monasteries in the Systems of Production and Exchange of the Frankish World Between the Seventh and the Ninth Centuries', in Inge Lyse Hansen and Chris Wickham (eds.), *The Long Eighth Century. Production, Distribution and Demand* (Leiden, 2000), pp. 123–39; Ian Wood, 'Before or After Mission. Social Relations across the Middle and Lower Rhine in the Seventh and Eighth Centuries', in Hansen and Wickham (eds.), *The Long Eighth Century*, pp. 149–66.

[7] Verhulst, 'Genèse du régime domanial classique'.

the regions between the Seine, Meuse and Rhine, approximately along an imaginary line between Paris and Aachen. This impression is based on the fact that at the edges of these areas, such as the delta of the Meuse and Rhine rivers or in Maine, in western France, as well as in little-exploited and densely wooded parts of the central regions themselves, such as the Ardennes in south-east Belgium or the Argonne forest in north-east France, the system was still in full development as late as the middle of the ninth century, and often was unable to mature fully. Obviously, this was even more true further afield in, for example, Thuringia. In contrast, the bipartite system had evolved centrally to such an extent that, primarily in the Paris region by the beginning of the ninth century, it showed signs of 'decline'. The only Mediterranean area in which the classical manorial system developed was in Italy after 774, and in fact it did so fully only in the north, especially in Lombardy.

On the basis of this chronological and geographical configuration, and given that the classical manorial system was mainly to be found on royal estates, on church lands that came from royal gifts and on estates of the high aristocracy who were often of royal blood as well, it may be that the system owed its existence, or at least its introduction, to the initiative of the Frankish king and his entourage. This does not exclude that some elements of the bipartite system existed already before its full formation, as studies on the gifts of land to St Germain-des-Prés, St Bertin and St Gall abbeys have shown. Conversely, this would explain why it hardly existed in the Carolingian period in the area between the Loire and the Pyrenees, brought within the Carolingian sphere of influence only late in the eighth century.[8]

THE EVOLUTION TOWARDS THE CLASSICAL MANOR

At the beginning of the development there was a type of exploitation that, during the Merovingian period, must have been present in almost all parts of western Europe.[9] This consisted of an estate

---

[8] Adriaan Verhulst, 'La diversité du régime domanial entre Loire et Rhin à l'époque carolingienne' in Janssen and Lohrmann (eds.), *Villa–Curtis–Grangia*, pp. 133–48; Adriaan Verhulst, 'Etude comparative du régime domanial classique à l'est et à l'ouest du Rhin à l'époque carolingienne', in *La croissance agricole* (Flaran 10), pp. 87–101; both articles were reprinted in Verhulst, *Rural and Urban Aspects*.

[9] Marie-Jeanne Tits-Dieuaide, 'Grands domaines, grandes et petites exploitations en Gaule mérovingienne', in Verhulst (ed.), *Le grand domaine*, pp. 23–50; Dieter Hägermann, 'Einige Aspekte der Grundherrschaft in den fränkischen formulae und in den leges des Frühmittelalters', *ibid.*, pp. 51–77.

or agricultural enterprise of from about 40 to 150 hectares of arable land, directly cultivated by slaves, who had no holding and lived on or near the centre of the estate. We may call it a 'demesne-centred' estate (Germ. *Gutsbetrieb*). If a few holdings were administered from within this centre they were in any case limited in numbers and obliged to provide only supplies and payments, not services. These domains were often situated in under-exploited areas, where they often played a pioneering role. In such cases, stock breeding, especially of pigs, became very important. Examples of this type can be found among the estates of the abbey of Fulda in central Germany at the beginning of the ninth century, among the possessions of the abbey of Montiérender in the Argonne forest in north-east France, and in Italy among the lands of the abbey of Farfa at the estuary of the Po, as well as in the mountainous regions of Piemonte and the central Appennines.[10]

In these large Italian farms, often simply called *curtes*, some holdings may have been included or their number extended. This could be done by assigning part of the demesne either to freed or unfree slaves as has been observed as early as the eighth century in some places in Italy, or by assigning not yet exploited parts of the demesne to new holdings. This is known to have been carried through in Italy as late as the second half of the ninth century. Between 862 and 883, the dates of two different stages of the polyptych of Bobbio, the number of holdings increased from 74 to 123. The complex that was henceforth often called *villa* rather than *curtis* had in this way evolved into a bipartite manor. Because slaves were still used on the demesne, the new holdings were not always made serviceable to the demesne upon their integration. Many factors were at work in the development of this type of organisation, among them the legal status of the tenant, the origin of the holding, the needs of the lord and the balance of power between his authority and the resistance of his subjects.

The first mentions of services, not of antique origin, are from the late sixth century. At the beginning of the eighth century they were fully developed, even in regions as far away from the centre of the Frankish kingdom as Bavaria, where they were regulated in a famous

---

[10] Ulrich Weidinger, 'Untersuchungen zur Grundherrschaft des Klosters Fulda in der Karolingerzeit', in Werner Rösener (ed.), *Strukturen der Grundherrschaft im frühen Mittelalter* (Göttingen, 1989), pp. 247–65; Ulrich Weidinger, *Untersuchungen zur Wirtschaftsstruktur des Klosters Fulda in der Karolingerzeit* (Stuttgart, 1991); Droste, *Polyptichon Montiérender*, p. 143; Pierre Toubert, 'L'Italie rurale aux VIIIe–IXe siècles', pp. 105–6.

article (I, 13) of the *Lex Baiuwariorum* ('De colonis vel servis ecclesiae, qualiter serviant vel qualia tributa reddant').[11]

A much debated problem involves the extent to which the big estate integrated independent peasants with their farm and hence the question of its representativity.[12] Some ninth-century holdings in certain manors of the abbey of St Bertin in north-west France, appearing to be small manors, have been considered by Morimoto as remnants of formerly independent peasant farms. This interpretation has been contested and these small manors have been interpreted by Renard as *beneficia* or *precaria*. This means that the gift of an independent peasant of his farm to the abbey was retroceded to him, augmented with land out of the abbey's possession.

The integration or creation of holdings did not always lead to a bipartite estate. When holdings were scattered over several villages, for example, next to and among lands of other lords, the demesne court, exploited with the help of a number of slaves, simply became a rent-collecting centre, with no additional links to the holdings. Examples of this type can be found among the possessions of Corvey, Fulda and, at the end of the ninth century, on certain possessions of the church of Lucca consisting of holdings (*sortes*) that were granted in *beneficium* as a whole and only yielded payments in money for the holder of the *beneficium*.[13] Royal initiative alone, even if also promoted and applied by the Carolingian church, was obviously insufficient to integrate big farms that had been cultivated directly by slaves, or small enterprises that had been more or less independent, into single large estates that were to be exploited in a different way from then onwards. For this

[11] E. von Schwind (ed.), *Monumenta Germaniae Historica Leges* 5, 2 (Hanover, 1926), pp. 286–90; Theodore J. Rivers, 'Seigneurial Obligations and "Lex Baiuvariorum" I, 13', *Traditio. Studies in Ancient and Medieval History, Thought and Religion* 31 (1975), pp. 336–43; Theodore J. Rivers, 'The Manorial System in the Light of the Lex Baiuvariorum', *Frühmittelalterliche Studien* 25 (1991), pp. 89–95. Complete text and German translation in Ludolf Kuchenbuch, *Grundherrschaft im früheren Mittelalter* (Idstein, 1991), pp. 95–6.

[12] Morimoto, 'Autour du grand domaine carolingien', pp. 69–70; Etienne Renard, 'Lectures et relectures d'un polyptyque carolingien (Saint-Bertin 844–859)', *Revue d'histoire ecclésiastique* 94 (1999), pp. 392–406.

[13] Corvey abbey: Werner Rösener, 'Zur Struktur und Entwicklung der Grundherrschaft in Sachsen in karolingischer und ottonischer Zeit', in Verhulst (ed.), *Le grand domaine*, pp. 200–3; Fulda abbey: Weidinger, 'Untersuchungen zur Grundherrschaft', pp. 256–8; Lucca abbey: Pierre Toubert, 'Il sistema curtense: la produzione e lo scambio interno in Italia nei secoli VIII, IX e X', in *Storia d'Italia. Annali 6: Economia naturale, economia monetaria* (Turin, 1983), p. 27.

system to be introduced more or less completely, and for it to be exploited more or less efficiently, still other factors must have been at work. Reclamation of wooded but fertile soils, usually covered with loess, enlarged the amount of arable land in the demesne, often in the form of extensive homogeneous and compact agricultural complexes called *culturae* between the Seine and the Rhine and *territoria* in central Germany.[14] They were the result of the labour not only of serfs who lived on the demesne without their own farms, but also of free and semi-free newcomers. In exchange, these people of diverse origins and status were allowed to cultivate a small part of the unexploited part of the demesne for themselves and to keep it as a holding. They were obliged to make payments and provide supplies and they had to render agricultural services to the lord to help out on the enlarged demesne, which in this way could muster added labour. Obviously, all this was only possible on extensive estates and those were largely in the hands of the king, bishoprics, monasteries and the aristocracy. An additional beneficial factor of the establishment of a classical bipartite exploitation scheme was the concentration of ownership and the location of those possessions in the vicinity of the owners' power centres, that is the royal palaces, the bishops' cities and the abbeys.

POLYPTYCHS, INVENTORIES AND THEIR AIMS

This largely abstract and ideal model of the classical manorial structure and the history of its origins and expansion can be made more concrete by means of extant management documents and inventories (*polyptyca, descriptiones, brevia*), which almost without exception date back to the ninth century and usually form part of an ecclesiastical archive, nearly always in a later copy. Only the most famous and very complete polyptych from the Paris abbey of St Germain-des-Prés, drawn up by order of its abbot Irmino shortly before 829, is preserved in its original form. Other famous polyptychs are, in chronological order:[15] those of the abbeys of St Victor de Marseilles (813–14), Wissembourg (before 818–19), Montiérender (before 845), St Bertin (844–59), St Remi de Reims (after 848), Bobbio (862 and 883),

---

[14] Cf. Chapter 1 (footnote 14) and Chapter 4.

[15] Cf. Introduction: footnotes 20 and 21; Chapter 2 footnote 1 and A. Castagnetti, M. Luzatti, G. Pasquali and A.Vasina (eds.), *Inventari altomedievali di terre, coloni e redditi* (Rome, 1979: Fonti per la Storia d'Italia 104).

Lobbes (868–9), St Maur-des-Fossés (869–78), Prüm (893). In most of these, the lord, mostly an abbot, had had recorded the composition of the demesne in terms of land, buildings, personnel and infrastructure, but more particularly the obligations of the tenants with respect to services, deliveries of supplies and payments, thus showing the potentialities of his possessions. Fragments of *Breve* XV *de Villanova* in the polyptych of St Germain-des-Prés by abbot Irmino illustrate this:[16]

C.1. The abbey has in Villeneuve one demesne (*mansum indominicatum*) with a house and other edifices in sufficient number; of arable land 172 *bunuaria*, which can take 800 *modios* of grain for sowing. There are 91 *aripennos* of vineyard from which 1,000 *modii* can be collected; 166 *aripennos* of meadow from which 166 carts of hay may be gathered. There are 3 mills (*farinarios*) from which 450 *modios* of grain have come as rent. Another mill is not given out at rent. There is woodland 4 leagues in circumference, where 500 pigs can be fed. C.2. There is a church, well constructed, with all its furniture and with a house and other buildings in sufficient quantity. To it belong 3 holdings (*mansi*). The priest and his dependants have 27 *bunuaria* of arable and 1 *ancinga*, 17 *aripennos* of vineyard and 25 of meadow. From this holding one horse is delivered as gift. Nine *perticas* and one *ancinga* of the demesne (*ad opus dominicum*) and 2 *perticas* of the field to be sown with spring corn (*ad tremissum*) must be ploughed; 4 *perticas* of meadow have to be enclosed. C.3. Actardus, a *colonus*, and his wife Eligildis, a *colona*, dependants of St Germain, have living with them 6 children whose names are Ageteus, Teudo, Simeon, Adalsida, Deodata, Electarda. They are holding one *mansus ingenuilis*, having 5 *bunuaria* of arable and 2 *antsingas*, 4 *aripennos* of vineyard and four and a half *aripennos* of meadow. They pay 4 *solidi* of silver for military service (*ad hostem*) one year, 2 *solidi* instead of delivering animals for the army (*carnaticum*) in the second year and for herbage tax (*herbaticum*) in the third year one sheep with its lamb. They pay 2 *modios* wine for grazing tax (*in pastione*), 4 pennies for woodcutting (*lignaricia*), one foot (*pedalem*) of (wood) transport (*carratio*), 50 shingles. He ploughs 4 *perticas* to be sown with winter corn (*ad hibernaticum*), 2 *perticas* to be sown with spring corn (*ad tremisso*). Services (*curvatas*), handiwork services (*manopera*) as many as are imposed upon him. He delivers 4 chickens, 15 eggs, and encloses 4 *perticas* of meadow.

C.84. Aclebertus and his wife Frotlindis, an unfree woman (*ancilla*), both dependants of St Germain, have one child named Acleburg. Teutfridus, a serf

---

[16] D. Hägermann (ed.), *Das Polyptychon von Saint-Germain-des-Prés*, pp. 129–38. (Adapted with corrections from the translation in Roy C. Cave and Herbert H. Coulson (eds.), *A Source Book for Medieval Economic History*, reprint edition, (New York, 1963), pp. 43–4, and part of Paul Halsall (ed.), *Internet Medieval Source Book*, 1988).

(*servus*) of St Germain, has his mother with him. These two hold together one *mansus servilis*, having 4 *bunuaria* of arable, one *aripennum* of vineyard, 4 *aripennos* of meadow. Its obligations are the same [as those enumerated under C.76 being the first of C.76 to C.90, most of which concern tenants of *mansi serviles*:] he has to work 4 *aripennos* in the vineyard (of the demesne), pays 3 *modios* wine for grazing tax (*in pascione*), one *sestarius* of mustard, 50 osier bundles, 3 chickens, 15 eggs. Handiwork services when and where they are imposed on them. And the unfree woman has to make a cloth from wool of the demesne and doughs (*pastas*) so many as she is ordered to.

In principle, the surveys of fiefs (*beneficia*) and possessions held as *precaria*, the income of which was not directly to the benefit of the lord, were also noted down in such documents, but few of these survive. In spite of their similarities, there was no stereotype conception of a polyptych. Besides them other documents showed the composition of the landed possessions of a mostly ecclesiastical lord. Some are simple lists, others are pure inventories of the demesne – its acreage, equipment, stocks, etc. – and only give totals of the numbers of holdings, sometimes with their produce. The survey of the landed possessions of the abbey of Fontenelle / St Wandrille (bishopric of Rouen), around 787, serves as an example:[17]

This is the sum of the possessions of this abbey, which were enumerated by order of the most invincible King Charles in the twentieth year of his reign by abbot Landricum of Gemmeticum and count Richard, in the year of the death of abbot [Witlaicus].

First those (possessions) which are for the own use and allowance of the monks: 1,313 full *mansi* (*mansi integri*), 238 half *mansi* and 18 *mansi* obliged to handiwork services (*mansi manoperarii*) were counted, totalling 1,569, 158 unoccupied *mansi* (*mansi absi*) and 39 mills. In fief are given 2,120 *mansi integri*, 40 half *mansi* and 235 *mansi manoperarii*, totalling 2,395 and 156 unoccupied *mansi*. The tenants of fiefs have 28 mills. The sum of all the present possessions (counting whole, half and handiwork *mansi*) is 4,264, except those manors which [Witlaicus] gave to the king's men or in usufruct to others.

The most famous of such inventories is the description of several royal domains near Lille in northern France, of which Annappes was the centre, dating from the first years of the ninth century, and of which a fragment was quoted above.[18] The presence in the same manuscript of the famous regulation of Charlemagne for the royal estates, known

[17] F. Lohier and R. P. J. Laporte (eds.), *Gesta Sanctorum Fontanellensis coenobii* (Rouen, Paris, 1936), pp. 82–3.

[18] Footnote 5.

as the *Capitulare de Villis*, and some formulary-like elements of the text suggest that this inventory was intended as a model for similar inquiries.[19] Hence its editor gave it the name of *Brevium exempla*, but it is not clear whether it actually ever had that function. The variety of motives for redaction and hence of many elements of the texts are too great to support such a hypothesis. This does not mean that the king did not urge the churches to draw up such documents. Some ordinances in capitularies prove the opposite.

These managerial documents at first sight present no picture of evolution unless a similar document of some decades later has been preserved, as in the rare case of Bobbio (with records for 862 and 883).[20] Indeed, the purpose of these documents was primarily to determine the obligations of the inhabitants of the estate, probably after consultation and in agreement with them, in order to be able to standardise and in this way optimise the structure and exploitation of the estate. Even then, this normalisation took place separately from estate to estate, or in terms of geographical grouping of estates, which means that in spite of a certain common basic structure, which the lord attempted to introduce through the elaboration of these managerial documents, a great variety can still be observed. This variety is often determined regionally.

Examples of this can be found among the possessions of the abbey of St Germain-des-Prés as registered in Abbot Irmino's polyptych. Those situated in the Perche region, south-west of Paris, have characteristics that are very different from those in the Île-de-France around Paris. Corbon (*Breve* XII) is one of the most typical.[21] As an abbey estate it originated not by a royal gift of a compact manor, like many manors around Paris, but by many smaller individual gifts of *mansi* of mostly three or four *bunuaria* situated in a village (*villa*) and sometimes of hamlets, of which some had a bipartite structure and thus a demesne. There was no central demesne, but many peasant farms had a standard acreage of 3 to 5 hectares. Another atypical element of the Corbon estate were the plots won from the forest *ad medietatem*. This means in exchange for half their production, a type of holding to be used on a larger scale some centuries later. In the nearby manor of Boissy-Maugis (dép. Orne, ar. Mortagne-au-Perche) similar small *villae*-hamlets, each having scattered small arable fields called *culturae*,

[19] Verhein, 'Studien Reichsgut'.   [20] Castagnetti, *Inventari*.
[21] Hägermann (ed.), *Polyptychon Saint-Germain-des-Prés*, pp. 98–103.

were at the time of Irmino's polyptych already regrouped into larger units under *ministri*.[22]

The lord's initiative was, however, limited not only because of geographic differences such as the presence or not of extensive loess plateaux, mountains, infertile soils, woods or bogs, but also as a result of pre-existing economic and social structures, especially as far as the legal status of large parts of the population was concerned (with possible groups of freemen, freed men, half-free *coloni* or slaves). This variety, as demonstrated by both estates of St Germain-des-Prés in western France, makes it hardly sensible to describe one concrete domain as the ideal example of a classical bipartite estate, even though a manor of the abbey of St Germain-des-Prés from the immediate vicinity of Paris, such as Palaiseau, is often taken as a model for it. That is why we limit the following description to some general characteristics of the directly exploited part of the estate – the demesne – on the one hand, and those of the holdings on the other hand.

THE DEMESNE

The demesne consisted of various kinds of uncultivated as well as arable land. The latter could extend to several hundred hectares, the woodland to thousands. The arable land of the demesne of Palaiseau, for example, consisted of 396 hectares and was one of the largest among the demesnes of St Germain-des-Prés, the arable land of which generally amounted to between 200 and 300 hectares. The arable land of the demesnes of the abbey of St Bertin was somewhat less extensive, between 200 and 250 hectares. This is on average still two to three times as much as on the estates of Montiérender, which were situated some 150 km to the east of Paris and were still in full expansion as classical estates in the ninth century, mainly through deforestation.[23] The Paris estates of St Germain-des-Prés had arable land most of which had been in use before the advent of the Carolingians, but much of it originated through reclamations during the seventh and eighth centuries. The latter had come to an end on most estates of St Germain-des-Prés at the time of Irmino's polyptych (*c.* 825–9). Some large demesnes elsewhere, however, with

---

[22] *Ibid.*, pp. 104–19.
[23] Claus-Dieter Droste, 'Die Grundherrschaft Montiérender im 9. Jahrhundert', in Verhulst (ed.), *Le grand domaine*, pp. 101–11; Patrick Corbet (ed.), *Les moines du Der 673–1790* (Langres, 2000).

less arable, but including vast areas of wooded land, carried out reclamations well into the ninth century. This was particularly the case
around the middle of the ninth century on several manors of the
abbey of Montiérender. Four had woodland for a thousand pigs,
which amounts more or less to 1,000 hectares per manor, although
the acreage could fluctuate from nearly 1 to nearly 3 hectares per pig.
The total number of pigs at Montiérender was nearly 9,000, three
times more than at St Germain-des-Prés. New holdings were created at Montiérender on wooded demesne land and given out at
one-eleventh of their output, a totally different system from that of
the *mansus*. On certain estates of royal origin to the east of the Rhine,
the acreage of arable land within the demesne was five times as extensive as the average acreage of 40 to 50 hectares on less classical
domains both in Bavaria and in Saxony. The 250 to 300 hectares of
arable on the demesne of the bishop of Augsburg at Staffelsee in south
Bavaria are a rather exceptional example.[24]

Depending on the geographical conditions, the arable land of the
demesne could largely be concentrated in extensive *culturae*, in which
case the latter were not very numerous, or they could be distributed
over a large number of smaller *culturae* or *territoria* (as on the estate
of the abbey of Prüm in Villance in the Belgian Ardennes),[25] without ever being mixed with the individual fields of the tenants. The
latter situation, the so-called *Gemengelage*, was mainly to be found
in the border areas of the classical estate (western France, Saxony,
Rheinhessen).

From an economic point of view, the proportion between the total
area of the demesne and that of the holdings is important. It provides
us with an indication of the number of labourers required for the
cultivation of the demesne. The larger the area of arable land in the
demesne the more labour was required. In evenly developed classical
estates the proportion between demesne and holdings was around
1:2.5 and 1:3, as was the case on the estates of St Germain-des-Prés,
Lorsch[26] and the Staffelsee estate between 800 and 820[27] and on the

[24] Verhulst, 'Etude comparative'.
[25] Schwab, *Prümer Urbar*, pp. 94–7; Etienne Renard, 'La gestion des domaines
    d'abbaye aux viiie–xe siècles', *De la Meuse à l'Ardenne* 29 (1999), pp. 117–50.
[26] Verhulst, 'Etude comparative', p. 95; Franz Staab, 'Aspekte der Grundherrschaft-
    sentwicklung von Lorsch vornehmlich aufgrund der Urbare des Codex Laures-
    hamensis', in Rösener (ed.), *Strukturen der Grundherrschaft*, pp. 305–34.
[27] Verhulst, 'Etude comparative', p. 93; Konrad Elmshäuser, 'Untersuchungen zum
    Staffelseer Urbar', in Rösener (ed.), *Strukturen der Grundherrschaft*, pp. 335–69.

former *fiscus* Friemersheim on the lower Rhine around 890.[28] On some manors of St Bertin the proportion was somewhat lower, about 1:1.5 or 1:1.75 or 1:2.

Because of the large extent of arable land in the demesne on some estates the proportion between demesne and tenures could sometimes rise to 1:1, as was the case on some domains of royal provenance belonging to the abbey of Wissembourg.[29] For the exploitation of such relatively large demesnes the rather onerous services of the tenants were no longer sufficient. It must therefore be assumed that even on these classical estates fairly heavy use was made of resident slaves without holdings. This can be proved in some cases, as at Staffelsee, where in spite of a basic service of three days a week by slaves who were housed on nineteen *mansi serviles* and who in addition cultivated 17 per cent of the fields of the demesne in plots according to the system of the *riga/ancinga*, there were an additional seventy-two *provendarii* without holdings at the disposal of the demesne. In a more general sense this was also the case on most of the still expanding estates of Montiérender shortly before 845, where on average thirteen slaves can be counted per demesne, especially on the smaller domains that were given in *precaria*.

The data concerning the smaller estate units of the aristocracy in various regions of Germany, such as Saxony and Bavaria, also indicate that the smaller the manors, the more use of resident slaves was made for the exploitation of the demesne.[30] The exploitation of the demesne by means of services by tenants therefore seems to have been a system that was mainly developed on large estates, usually owned by the king or donated by him. A typical example of this is the abbey of Fulda. Here only estates with demesnes of more than 150 hectares of arable land were organised according to a bipartite system and largely dependent on the services of tenants for their exploitation.[31]

THE HOLDINGS, ESPECIALLY THE *MANSUS*

Certain rights were attached to the holding in exchange for payments to the lord, both in kind and in money, and for services on his

---

[28] Verhulst, 'Etude comparative', p. 92.   [29] Dette, *Liber possessionum*, pp. 54–7.

[30] Werner Rösener, 'Strukturformen der adeligen Grundherrschaft in der Karolingerzeit', in Rösener (ed.), *Strukturen der Grundherrschaft*, pp. 158–67.

[31] Weidinger, 'Untersuchungen zur Grundherrschaft', pp. 251–65.

demesne. Only in the course of the ninth century did rents and services sometimes come to be fixed with regard to the personal juridical status of the tenant, instead of on the original free or unfree status of their holding, as on the estates of St Bertin abbey in northern France.[32] This means that in this case the person of the tenant, more particularly his legal status of free, freed, half-free or slave, played a role in the imposition on his holding of service obligations, especially regarding size and nature.

In the second half of the seventh century, the term *mansus* appears for the first time in the region of Paris, as a new technical term for a holding. A *mansus* then consisted not only of a farmhouse and farm buildings (*mansio*), but also of fields and sometimes also meadows. Its introduction might have been related to the development of the classical, bipartite manorial system based on services. The Frankish kings might indeed have played as important a role in the introduction of the use of the term *mansus* as they had in the rise of the bipartite manorial system. This is suggested by the spread of the use of the term *mansus*, from the Paris region in all directions corresponding to the region in which the manorial system developed in its classical form. In most regions *mansus* replaced older terms such as *coloni(c)a, casata, factus* and *hoba*, although *coloni(c)a* and *factus* continued to exist to the south of the Loire with their simple original meaning of a holding not necessarily being part of a larger domanial unit.[33] *Casata* and *hoba* were retained in Germanic-speaking areas, often with the same meaning as *mansus*,[34] but sometimes not, as the special evolution at Fulda shows. Here, in around 830, *mansus* meant the central building of a small farm, whereas *hoba* was used for all lands belonging to it. Such *mansi*, in the sense of small houses, were created for the settlement of slaves, who would continue working on the demesne.[35]

Mansus, essentially (and more specifically in polyptychs), came to mean a unit of assessment for payments, in kind and money and for services. The Frankish king, from the end of the eighth century onwards, also began to use it for fiscal and related matters, for example

[32] Ganshof, *Polyptyque Saint-Bertin*, p. 32.
[33] Fournier, *Peuplement rural en Basse-Auvergne*, pp. 241–2.
[34] Walter Schlesinger, 'Die Hufe im Frankenreich', in Hans Patze and Fred Schwind (eds.), *Ausgewählte Aufsätze von W. Schlesinger 1965–1979* (Sigmaringen, 1987), pp. 587–614.
[35] Weidinger, *Untersuchungen zur Wirtschaftsstruktur*, pp. 23–38.

to determine the military obligations of his vassals.[36] After the middle of the ninth century *mansus* (now also spelled as *mansum*, plural *mansa*) was also used to express the acreage of demesne land, formerly expressed in *buonaria*, *iugera* or *iurnales*, and for rough estimates of the value of some land or of whole regions. It was also used by the king as a basis for various taxes. This is why some modern authors consider it a purely fiscal unit, which they trace back, incorrectly in my view, to the Roman taxation system that persisted here and there in the Merovingian period.[37] The problem is that the *mansus* is no fixed unit, either in terms of area or in terms of the charges and obligations connected with it, although the normal occupancy of a *mansus* is supposed to be by one tenant and its legal size twelve *b(u)onarii* (16.5 hectares). In estates where the *mansus* organisation seems to be fairly recent the areas of the *mansi* are rather large, as is the case on the estate of Poperinge near Ypres, belonging to the abbey of St Bertin, in about the middle of the ninth century. They constitute groups in which all the *mansi* have an area of 24, 20, 15 or 13 bonniers, thus pointing to a systematic origin by a creation from the abbey.[38] In Palaiseau, a *villa* near Paris of the abbey of St Germain-des-Prés, where the arable land and its organisation within a manor are of much older origin, the size of the *mansi* is much smaller. It is by no means certain that there is a connection with the so-called overpopulation of the *mansus*, in which the latter was inhabited by more than one family. This was the case with half the total number of *mansi* at Palaiseau.

THE CHARGES OF THE *MANSUS*, ESPECIALLY LABOUR SERVICES

As far as payments in kind and money or labour services are concerned, it is even more difficult to distinguish specific, let alone standard, types.[39] What does occur is that within one particular estate all *mansi* of a category (that may or may not have been juridically

---

[36] F. L. Ganshof, *Frankish Institutions under Charlemagne* (New York, 1970: Norton Library), pp. 52 and 60–1.

[37] J. Durliat, *Les finances publiques de Dioclétien aux Carolingiens (284–889)* (Sigmaringen, 1990: Beihefte der Francia 21), pp. 195–203.

[38] Ganshof, *Polyptyque St Bertin*, pp. 130–1.

[39] Ludolf Kuchenbuch, 'Probleme der Rentenentwicklung in den klösterlichen Grundherrschaften des frühen Mittelalters', in W. Lourdeaux and D. Verhelst (eds.), *Benedictine Culture 750–1050* (Leuven, 1983), pp. 130–72.

defined) were subject to the same obligations, which meant that
these obligations had to be entered only once in the chapter of the
polyptych concerned. Such uniformity occurs mainly in the case of
mansi serviles, as, for example, on the manor of Staffelsee belonging to
the bishop of Augsburg.[40] It may be explained by the fact that *mansi
serviles* were usually created anew and that it was easier to impose
uniform obligations on slaves than on free or half-free *coloni*. The
holdings of the latter may indeed have been previously independent
farms that had been integrated in an estate only later, in which case
an agreement had possibly to be concluded with the free person or
colonus concerned. This difference in juridical status might also explain the fact that *mansi serviles* or *servi* personally were usually taxed
much more heavily in services than *lidi*, *coloni* or *ingenui*. On most
bipartite estates in the Frankish regions to the east of the Rhine the
lowest burden of field work of the *mansi serviles* was two to three days
a week, in addition to other labour services. On top of that, they
often had to be available for service at any moment, whenever they
were ordered.[41]

Services fixed by days or weeks per year, fifteen days or 'nights'
('XV *dies*', 'XV *noctes*'), were very often linked to the free status of
the tenant. The cultivation, the whole year through, of a plot of
the demesne for the lord's profit, the so-called 'piecework' (Lat. *riga*,
ancinga), was also typical for free tenants,[42] although here and there,
for example at the Staffelsee manor of the bishop of Augsburg, unfree
tenures (*mansi serviles*) were charged with it.

At the big manor of Friemersheim in Westphalia, belonging to the
abbey of Werden on the river Ruhr, all peasant farms had to perform
three times for two weeks (*noctes*) per year, along with the cultivation
of an *ancinga*. But in the same region labour services on possessions
of the abbey of Prüm amounted to two days per week. The difference between the two systems could at first sight be ascribed to
different ownership but might rather be related, according to another
interpretation, to a different structure of the manor and to the density of possessions of an owner in the neighbourhood.[43] Whichever

---

[40] Elmshäuser, 'Staffelseer Urbar', p. 365.
[41] Verhulst, 'Étude comparative', pp. 93, 96, 98; Kuchenbuch, 'Rentenentwicklung'.
[42] Charles-Edmond Perrin, 'De la condition des terres dites "ancingae"', in *Mélanges
Ferdinand Lot* (Paris, 1925); J. F. Niermeyer, *Mediae Latinitatis Lexicon Minus*
(Leiden, 1976), p. 43, v° *andecinga*.
[43] Hans-Werner Goetz, 'Herrschaft und Raum in der frühmittelalterlichen Grundherrschaft', *Annalen des Historischen Vereins für den Niederrhein* 190 (1987), pp. 7–33.

is the case, this difference is a strong argument against the regional typology that Kuchenbuch thinks possible to detect among tenants' obligations on the manors of the abbey of Prüm.[44] Such regional differences are nevertheless clearly discernible when comparing the estates of St Germain-des-Prés around Paris with those in western France.

One could conclude with Goetz[45] that the internal structure of a manor influenced peasant charges, that regional customs existed but in a very loose manner, with intraregional differences, and that the origin of the possession is important. Generally, indeed, the original structure was not immediately changed by the new lord, and some elements of it usually persisted. The general tendency during the ninth century, however, was for more precise and limited labour services, not necessarily in the sense of a lightening of the charges, as can be observed in the opposite sense between 816–25 and 848 on the possessions of St Remi de Reims.[46]

In the regions to the east of the Rhine and in Italy as well as in some areas to the west of the realm such as the Argonne forest around the abbey of Montiérender, the services required of free and half-free tenants were normally limited to some transport services, to agricultural services during a few periods of two weeks (*noctes*) in the year and to the cultivation of a fixed plot of the demesne. This limitation was possible because there were many slaves available. In the western part of the realm in the ninth century, on the other hand, the number of slaves had been severely reduced, probably because of the process of settling them on holdings. This process in its turn had obscured the difference in social position between these former slaves and the free and half-free tenants within the same estate. The difference between, for instance, the *mansi ingenuiles* and the *mansi serviles* had thus largely disappeared in these regions. To ensure the exploitation of large demesnes, free and half-free tenants in the western part of the realm were therefore requested to perform practically the same services as slaves elsewhere. This presupposes a strong hold on the population by the authority of the king and the church, but may, on the other hand, be due to the heavy population pressure discussed above. Hence the possibility for the lord to change the tenant's labour obligations, as can be particularly well observed on the estates of St Remi de Reims and St Bertin. On the latter it was

---

[44] Kuchenbuch, 'Rentenentwicklung'.   [45] Goetz, 'Herrschaft und Raum'.
[46] *Ibid.*, pp. 27–9.

in the sense of unification, although the difference between free and unfree continued in the difference between the two days' service of the free and the three days' service of the unfree. On the estates of St Remi the diminution of unfree labour attached to the manorial centre was paralleled by the growing importance of labour services and the expansion of tenant land.

Polyptychs reflect these bipolar relations between an offensive lordship and the defensive peasantry, depending on the relative power of both. Lordship power was not possible without at least the passive consent or resignation of the peasantry and, sometimes, even their participation. Interventions by the king or by other authorities in these matters were not excluded: in 800, in a capitulary for the region of Le Mans in western France, Charlemagne regulated services after a complaint by peasants of both ecclesiastical and royal estates, in the following way:[47]

Every man holding a quarter of a *factus*, must be ploughing his lord's land a whole day with his beasts and thereafter his lord may not ask him to do handiwork service during the same week. And he who has not enough beasts to do this in one day shall complete the work in two days; and he who has only four infirm beasts, incapable of ploughing by themselves, has to join other beasts in order to plough the lord's land in one day and thereafter shall do one day of handiwork services in that week. And he who cannot do anything of these and has no draught-animals shall work three days (in a week) with his hands for his lord from dawn until sunset and his lord shall not ask more from him. In different ways this was happening indeed: some worked the whole week, some half a week, some two days. Therefore we have decided that the dependants shall not withdraw from these services and that the lords shall not ask more from them.

In 858 archbishop Hincmar of Reims addressed a long letter to the bishops present at Quierzy concerning the relations between lords and peasants in which he insisted that the estate agents should not oppress the peasants, nor ask more from them than in earlier days.[48]

In contrast with many labour services, there was not any consistency in the payments in kind and money that *mansi*, as holdings in an estate, were required to perform. Nor was there any correlation between the payments, the size and, particularly, the status of the *mansus*, except in the case of the *hostilitium*, which was paid only by *mansi ingenuiles* to buy off military service due from free men. Other payments in money were insignificant before the end of the ninth century.

[47] Boretius (ed.), *Capitularia*, vol. I, no. 31, pp. 81–2.   [48] *Ibid.* no. 297, p. 437.

From that moment on some supplies in kind (e.g. pigs, wood or linen) were with increasing frequency bought off with annual payments in money. Most supplies or payments in kind consisted still of small quantities of chickens and eggs. Industrial products (made of wood or iron if the geographical area was rich in these raw materials) were only relatively common when no or few services were requested from the *mansi*. On certain estates of St Germain-des-Prés, mostly west and south-west of Paris, in Villemeux, Boissy and in others where the manorial organisation was less developed, objects in wood or iron had to be delivered to the abbey by artisans not integrated in the manor but still dependent on the abbey.[49] Grain rents were not very frequent because cereals were produced in sufficient quantities on the demesnes. Only exceptionally were they paid to the abbey of Prüm for tenements on the Lower Rhine, the Meuse and in Saxony, where there was no direct exploitation of a demesne. Many were paid for the replacement of other rents in kind or were themselves changed into money rents.[50]

NON-CLASSICAL MANORIAL FORMS

The classical manorial organisation was manifestly a phenomenon that was limited in time and space. Under the influence of various factors such as population increase, divisions of estates owned by the king and aristocracy, by means of enfeoffments, gifts, sales, inheritance and the expansion of trade and money, the relationship based on services between the demesne and holdings classified as *mansi* evolved. This is clear from various polyptychs of a later date or younger parts of them from the abbeys of Lobbes, Prüm, Reims and St Maur-des-Fossés. It is possible, therefore, to work out a chronologically and geographically determined typology of those manorial forms and structures that diverge from the classical model, even though they occurred in its range of distribution or at least at the edge of it.

As some examples from western France of estates diverging from the classical bipartite model have been dealt with earlier in this book in another context, non-classic manorial types from other regions of France will now be presented.

[49] Elmshäuser and Hedwig, *Studien Polyptychon St Germain-des-Prés*, pp. 492–4.
[50] Ludolf Kuchenbuch, *Bäuerliche Gesellschaft und Klosterherrschaft im 9. Jahrhundert. Studien zur Sozialstruktur der Familia der Abtei Prüm* (Wiesbaden, 1978), pp. 146–67.

Eastern France: pioneer farms of Montiérender

The estates of the abbey of Montiérender, situated east of Paris, between the rivers Aube and Marne, south of Champagne, are listed in the polyptych from shortly before 845.[51] Their exploitation centre (*mansus indominicatus*) was not much larger than an ordinary peasant farm (*mansus*). Its arable land had an acreage of 25 to 40 or 50 bonniers, a quarter of the arable land of the classic manors of St Germain-des-Prés. It was cultivated mainly by unfree landless people (*mancipia*), on average thirteen people per manor.[52] Five hundred to 1,000 pigs could be pastured in the woods belonging to the demesne, three times more than on estates of St Germain-des-Prés. Many manors had newly reclaimed land not divided into *mansi* but given out at the eleventh sheaf. Much deserted land was rented in the same way. Because of its very small exploitation centre – only 8 to 9 hectares of arable land – its numerous pigs (800) and only four dependent free peasant farms (*mansi ingenuiles*), Thilleux, 4 km south-east of Montiérender (Chapter V of the polyptych), belongs to a type that may be called a 'pioneer farm'. As on most other peasant farms of Montiérender, the few tenants were charged with light services, three times three days per year ploughing and other tillage work (*aratura, corvada, beneficia*), carriage and handwork (*carropera et manopera*), here and elsewhere mostly unlimited, fifteen days of unspecified work on the demesne and fifteen days in the abbey, transport service once a year (*ambascatio*), here unspecified but generally to the market of Châlons-sur-Marne or Langres (89 km away). The latter service could be bought off for ten pennies. Firewood (*lignare*) had to be delivered, one to five cart-loads per *mansus*, and wooden tiles (*scindulae*), here and on average one hundred per *mansus*. Hens (3 or 6) and eggs (15 or 30) had to be given and a relative high sum (one to three shillings) had to be paid as substitution for military service.

A particularity of the polyptych of Montiérender is the record of twelve manors at the end of the document held as *precaria* from the abbey. Because of this status they reflect in many ways the situation of the possessions of free men before they entered by gift into the abbey's patrimony. They may also be called 'pioneer farms' as they

[51] Droste, 'Grundherrschaft Montiérender'.
[52] Etienne Renard, 'Les *mancipia* carolingiens étaient-ils des esclaves? Les données du polyptyque de Montier-en-Der dans le contexte documentaire du ixe siècle', in Corbet (ed.), *Les moines du Der*, pp. 179–209.

were very active in land reclamation, had only tens of hectares of arable demesne land, few dependent *mansi*, but many unfree landless people.

Among the more than thirty manors of Montiérender the evolution from a small demesne-centred 'pioneer farm' to a more classic bipartite structure can be followed mainly by the extension of the demesne's arable land and the growing number of dependent *mansi* and newly reclaimed small dependent farms (*hospicia*).

The estates of Montiérender thus are an example of how within a regional type at the start determined by a forest landscape, the chronological stages towards a final classic bipartite cereal producing estate can be followed within one polyptych.

Northern France: St Bertin and the regularity of the mansus

A different picture emerges from the polyptych (844–59) of St Bertin's abbey near Saint-Omer in north-west France. Its estates, concentrated in the départements of Pas-de-Calais and Nord and over the Franco-Belgian border in Flemish-speaking Flanders, were situated in a region that already produced grain and had only scattered forests. Most of them were bipartite manors, of which many had the following particular features diverging from the classical manors of the Paris region. The *mansi*, without the normal qualification free (*ingenuiles*) or unfree (*serviles*), consist of groups within which all the *mansi* have the same size: seven manors out of twelve for example have *mansi* of 12 bonniers, the normal size of the 'official' *mansus integer* under Charlemagne and Louis the Pious. This regularity points to a recent creation or reorganisation.[53] Much land, however, is not organised as *mansi*: free people (*ingenui*) having residence exclusively on *mansi*, do not sit on land that has not yet been divided in *mansi*. The high number of non-tenants is striking. They bear different names: *luminarii*, *herescarii*, *lunarii*, *homines de duabus diebus in anno*. Their status and residence are not clear.[54] The first two categories are personally dependent from the abbey and probably live on land owned by the abbey. It is not certain that this is true for the two other categories, although they are in some way or another under the authority of the abbey for reasons unexplained until now. The most discussed aspect,

[53] Ganshof, *Polyptyque St Bertin*, pp. 129–31. [54] Renard, 'Lectures et relectures'.

however, of St Bertin's estate structure is the presence of small bipartite manors with the status of tenures within a large manor. Some historians consider them as pre-existing small manors that, at a certain moment, came into the hands of the abbey but preserved their original structure and mode of exploitation.[55] Others consider these small manors as new creations by the abbey, henceforth with the status of *beneficia* and as an endowment for some officers, who were mostly horsemen (*caballarii*) or even functioned as head of the manor (*major*).[56] In their internal structure, these small manors present the same regularity as the manor in which they are integrated, especially in the uniform size of the *mansi*. Some small manors are really bipartite and have two, three or four *mansi* working on a rather small demesne of 3.5 or 2.5 *mansi*, whereas the normal size of a demesne is 10.5 *mansi* and the average number of dependent *mansi* 18. Others have no dependent *mansi* at all and are 'demesne centred', with an arable demesne of 3.5 *mansi*, worked by unfree people (*mancipia*) for the tenant of the small manor or for the abbey's profit.

Southern France and north Spain: allodia

Let us now consider areas in France and adjacent Spain that were brought under Carolingian authority only late in the eighth century. These areas cannot be considered together. A distinction should be made between, on the one hand, Catalonia and Roussillon, about which there are fairly extensive if somewhat late sources,[57] and on the other, Auvergne, Charente, Poitou, the Limousin and Provence.[58] It is no coincidence that there are almost no documents available concerning manorial structures in these southern parts of France,

---

[55] Yoshiki Morimoto, 'Essai d'une analyse du polyptyque de l'abbaye de St. Bertin (milieu du ixe siècle)', *Annuario Instituto Giapponese di Cultura* 8 (1970–1), pp. 31–53.

[56] Ganshof, *Polyptyque Saint-Bertin*, pp. 45–9; Renard, 'Lectures et relectures', pp. 392–406.

[57] Pierre Bonnassie, 'La croissance agricole du haut moyen âge dans la Gaule du Midi et le Nord-Est de la péninsule ibérique', in *La croissance agricole* (Auch 1990: Flaran 10), pp. 13–35; Pierre Bonnassie, *La Catalogne autour de l'an mil*, second edition, 2 vols. (Paris, 1990).

[58] Fournier, *Peuplement rural en Basse Auvergne*; Ch. Lauranson-Rosaz, *L'Auvergne et ses marges (Vélay, Gévaudan) du VIIIe au XIe siècles* (Le Puy-en-Vélay, 1987); Monique Zerner, 'Sur la croissance agricole en Provence', in *La croissance agricole* (Auch 1990: Flaran 10), pp. 153–67.

except one or two polyptychs. The structure and exploitation of large landownership was indeed very different here from that of the classical manorial organisation, of which the polyptychs were the tools of operation *par excellence*. Outside Catalonia and Roussillon the main characteristics were firstly the prevalence of the small farm enterprise, usually in allodial property, or, as in the Auvergne, as tenements, and secondly the small size and significance of the demesne, cultivated directly for the lord by a few slaves, without services from holdings, for which the demesne was only a rent-collecting centre without any close links.

The numerous small *allodia* between the Loire and the Pyrenees may date from the late Roman period or may have originated through reclamations according to the system of the *aprisio*, which had a great success in Catalonia and Roussillon in the ninth and tenth centuries. The holdings owe their existence partly to the large-scale assignment of land to former slaves, as is apparent at the beginning of the ninth century from the polyptych of St Pierre-le-Vif, concerning Mauriac in the Central Massif in the south-west of the Auvergne.[59] Most of the holdings are much older and probably originated as possessions of late Roman *coloni*.

Their principal obligation consisted of the payment of a levy in kind that amounted to one-tenth of the harvest. It occurs in 672–6 under the name of *agrarium* in the oldest tax list of the abbey of St Martin in Tours[60] and is also mentioned in the seventh-century *Formulae Wisigothorum*. It was later converted to a fixed payment as in Mauriac in the Auvergne and at the beginning of the tenth century was still referred to with the telling name of *tasca*. Additionally, *colonicae* had to make payments for the right to pasture (*pascuarium*, *pasquier*). These consisted of one-tenth of the yield of cattle raised, chickens and eggs as oblations (*eulogiae*) and a *tributum* in money as a sign of dependence. A *colonica* had an average size of 16 hectares and could provide for the needs of one canon, which appears to make it similar to the *mansus* to the north of the Loire. The term *mansus*, however, began to be used to the south of the Loire only in the ninth century. First and foremost this occurred in the Auvergne, with a slightly divergent meaning, of which the exploitation of buildings, garden

---

[59] B. Phalip, 'La charte dite de Clovis', *Revue de la Haute-Auvergne* 1988, pp. 567–607; 1989, pp. 671–96.

[60] Shoichi Sato, 'L'*agrarium*: la charge paysanne avant le régime domanial, vie–viiie siècles', *Journal of Medieval History* 24 (1998), pp. 103–25.

and orchard in the immediate vicinity were the most important elements. Rarely or never did there exist an obligation for agricultural
services for the *mansus*. Elsewhere the term *mansus* was only found
in the meaning of seigneurial *mansus* (*chef-manse*), exploited directly
for the lord, as in Limousin.

In lower Catalonia, as well as in Roussillon, 80 to 90 per cent
of the land in the ninth and tenth centuries was taken up by the
allodial property of small peasants. Many of these *allodia*, however,
were transformed into holdings in the tenth and eleventh centuries
after they had been sold to large landowners. In exchange for part of
the yield, they became part of the large estates that were built up by
new, large abbeys from the ninth century onwards in the north-east
of the county of Barcelona (around Gerona and Ampurias) and in
Roussillon, as a result of the clearances of large forests and garrigues.
These most southern regions of the Frankish empire thus developed
in their own separate way.

Brittany

In the ninth century, landownership in Brittany consisted exclusively
of large or small *allodia*. When large-scale landownership became
important, especially that of abbeys such as Redon, the small *allodia*
were incorporated by gifts to the abbey and held from it in *precaria*.
The large *allodia* were mostly transformed into fiefs. Here again, as
in Catalonia and Roussillon, there appears to have been an abrupt
change from a society characterised by small peasant properties to
one dominated by large estates.[61]

Between the Meuse and the Rhine: Prüm

Manorial types in the lands between the Meuse and the Rhine can
best be studied through the polyptych of the abbey of Prüm (893),
because the latter's possessions were scattered over the whole region.[62]
Most of its manors were of the classical bipartite type and lay in the
Eifel between Prüm and the river Moselle and on the middle Rhine.
Different structures occurred at some distance from the abbey, at the

---

[61] André Chédeville and Noël-Yves Tonnerre, *La Bretagne féodale XIe–XIIIe siècle*
(Rennes, 1987), pp. 204–6.
[62] Schwab, *Prümer Urbar*; Kuchenbuch, *Bäuerliche Gesellschaft*; Kuchenbuch,
'Rentenentwicklung'.

edge of the core possessions, for example, in some isolated *mansi* near Liège on the Meuse and on the lower Rhine near Arnhem. They were of the rent-collecting type and had no or no very developed system of labour services, unlike other manors. They had to give grain, pigs and also money payments, which in some cases replaced rents in kind that had been bought off. The growing importance of money rents at the end of the ninth century is one of the non-classic characteristics, not only of those isolated possessions but also of other estates of Prüm, for example in the Ardennes. Other manors knew no money payments at all, especially not when situated in regions with no markets. Grain rents were transported to the abbey and to other centres of abbey administration for consumption, not to markets. Nor are there any traces of surplus sale at the seat of the abbey. Prüm offers evidence of contradictory aspects of progressive and conservative management. The abbey's wine trade on the Moselle river, supported by famous transport services on the river,[63] is an exception, and also the salt trade from Prüm's salines near Metz, which we describe in another chapter.

East of the Rhine

Not only were there notable differences between the structure and exploitation of estates west and east of the Rhine but the latter part of the Carolingian realm was itself diverse,[64] even if the basic structure was generally the same, that is to say either bipartite with labour services from holdings or in the form of a rent-collecting centre without services from the holdings. In both cases the demesne was not very large – some tens of hectares – and was worked, if really very small, by unfree *mancipia* or *servi* attached without a holding to the exploitation centre. When they were settled on a holding it was often a *mansus servilis*, charged with labour services of the three-days-per-week-type, to which, on some very large manors of royal origin, was added a plot of the demesne (*ancinga*) to cultivate the whole year through. East of the Rhine the free and half-free tenants were less numerous than the unfree. In Saxony it was mostly half-free *lidi*, a category that did not exist in Bavaria where in some parts *coloni*

---

[63] Jean-Pierre Devroey, 'Les services de transport à l'abbaye de Prüm au ixe siècle', *Revue du Nord* 61 (1979), pp. 543–69, reprinted in Devroey, *Etudes sur le grand domaine carolingien*.

[64] Verhulst, 'Etude comparative'; Rösener (ed.), *Strukturen der Grundherrschaft*.

were considered free. Their holdings, however, called *colonicae*, were mostly occupied by *servi* and *mancipia*. The normal type of holding, *mansus lidilis* in Saxony and *mansus ingenuilis* or *hoba* in Bavaria, was charged with labour services of the *noctes*-type, that is to say two weeks per year and thus relatively light, plus the cultivation of a fixed plot of the demesne. In Rheinhessen (Frankfurt region) *mansi ingenuiles*, more numerous than *mansi serviles*, and charged with four weeks per year instead of two elsewhere, were only to be found on fiscal land belonging to the crown, whereas the majority of the *mansi serviles* lay outside of the fiscs.

Classical bipartite estates, with numerous *mansi* and a geographically concentrated large demesne equal in size to the total sum of the holdings, were an exception east of the Rhine. They were mostly in the hands of the king or, when in ecclesiastical hands, of fiscal origin. Examples are: the former fisc of Friemersheim near Duisburg, belonging to the abbey of Werden, which had 400 hectares of arable demesne; the manor of Staffelsee in Bavaria, belonging to the bishop of Augsburg, with nearly 300 hectares; and the manor of Hammelburg in Thuringia, before its gift to Fulda by Charlemagne in 777 part of a royal estate on the middle Saale river, with more than 300 hectares of demesne arable and 660 dependent peasant farms. These manors, through an extension of the demesne by reclamations, incorporations and concentration, were ahead of an evolution towards a more classical bipartite structure that would, in the ninth century, affect many manors east of the Rhine whose situation until then had corresponded to that of most manors west of the Rhine in the seventh and eighth centuries. This evolution, because it implied an extension of the demesne, did not and could not take place without an increase in labour services, for the non-free tenants east of the Rhine and west of the Rhine for the free. This increase took place without notable peasant resistance, which in turn can probably be explained by demographic pressure. Perhaps this pressure was itself the result of a demographic growth caused by the settling of former slaves on holdings.

Italy

For Italy a manorial typology was worked out by Pierre Toubert[65] that reflects an evolution to the classical bipartite manor in much the

---

[65] Toubert, 'Italie rurale', 'Sistema curtense'.

same way as the evolution east of the Rhine just described. It is based on two criteria: the structure and exploitation of the demesne and the relation between demesne and holdings. Type I, characteristic for central Italy and the Po valley, is a so-called pioneer farm, without a structured demesne and a predominantly pastoral activity. Holdings owed no labour services but were engaged in reclamations. Type II had a structured demesne with mills and other installations. Cereals had only a secondary place in the production scheme, which was mainly oriented to olives and wine. Labour services were rare. The manor of Limonta in northern Italy is a well-known example of this type. Type III is the classical bipartite manor oriented to cereal production and often situated not far from the residence of the owner. It is characterised by the presence of extensive grain fields on good soils, called *culturae* and similar to those in north-west Europe. They were worked by the tenants' labour services.

In most cases of type I and II there was no strong link between demesne and holdings and labour services were rare and irregular. Cultivation of the demesne rested on the work of unfree *servi* and *prebendarii*, progressively settled on holdings taken out of the demesne. The possession of such peasant farms (*casa colonica*) hasted the merging of *coloni* and *servi*, especially in manors of type I, where new holdings were established on newly reclaimed soils at hard conditions of heavy labour services. This process went on until at least 820 to 840, which was the end of this colonisation period.

The Italian peasant farms were a much more flexible instrument of colonisation than the north-west European *mansus*. One of the reasons for this is the absence of interference with the personal status of the tenant. The *casa colonic(i)a* was well adapted to the narrow family and consequently was not exposed to partitions. The contrast of the loose settlement in Italy, especially in the Sabine region and the Po valley, with the rigid overpopulated *mansus* of the Paris region with its concentrated settlement, is striking.

SIGNS OF DECLINE OR GROWTH AND THE DESTINATION OF SURPLUSES

So far, I have referred to such indications of 'decline' as the over-population of the *mansus* and its small size on some estates of St Germain-des-Prés in the vicinity of Paris (like Palaiseau), with *mansi ingenuiles* of only two and three bonniers. Yet the case of the lands of the abbey of Prüm at Villance in the Belgian Ardennes proves that we have to be careful with the term 'decline'.[66] The overoccupation of four tenants per *mansus* on twenty-two of the thirty-five *mansi* at Villance cannot easily be interpreted as decline since it concerns a 'classical' estate that originated in the course of the ninth century as a result of clearances. In a similar way it has been possible to prove that the vacant *mansi* (*mansi absi*) that occurred in great numbers on the lands of the abbey of Montiérender *c.* 850 (around 20 per cent of the total number of *mansi ingenuiles*),[67] and the numerous *sortes absentes* that represented up to one-sixth of the total number of *sortes* in the mid-ninth and early tenth centuries in Italy (near cities this proportion was as high as 50 per cent),[68] were not 'abandoned' *mansi* or *sortes*, but holdings that had temporarily no official tenant and had been granted to other landholders. Their presence is evidence of great mobility within the domanial structures, to which the management of the estate could react with great flexibility because of the concept of 'vacant' holdings.

In the same way half *mansi* should not always be interpreted as the consequences of a division of a *mansus* and therefore as a sign of decline, but often as *mansi* in development, as was the case on some estates of St Bertin around 850. When, on the other hand, Charles the Bald complained in the Edict of Pîtres (864) that the *mansus* became ever smaller because essential elements of it had been alienated, this did concern in his opinion a process of decline, which even threatened the smooth operation of the state institutions.[69] The reduction of the demesne that can be observed mainly on some estates of the abbey of Bobbio from the middle of the ninth century onwards was a conscious policy aimed at multiplying the number of holdings and keeping alive a parallel and more intensive cultivation of a reduced demesne by means of the services created in this way. While here the phenomenon can be interpreted as an attempt at optimising efficiency, its general introduction on the estates of the abbeys of Prüm and Wissembourg

---

[66] See footnote 25 p. 42.
[67] Droste, *Polyptichon Montiérender*, p. 140; Renard, 'Mancipia carolingiens', p. 188; Jean-Pierre Devroey, 'Mansi absi: indices de crise ou de croissance de l'économie rurale du haut moyen âge', *Le Moyen Age* 82 (1976), pp. 421–51, reprinted in Devroey, *Grand domaine*.
[68] Toubert, 'Sistema curtense', p. 32.
[69] MGH Capit. II, no. 273, cc. 30, 31, pp. 323–4; Janet L. Nelson, *Charles the Bald* (London, 1992), p. 26.

at the end of the ninth and during the tenth century should probably indeed be interpreted as a decline of the classical domanial system.

The manorial system was at that time in fact clearly past its peak and it is possibly not without significance that its decline coincided with the reduction of royal authority. As argued above, the original development of the manorial system had clearly been linked to the rise and expansion in all senses of the power of the Carolingian rulers, and may even have been a component of a 'Carolingian agrarian policy'. The promotion of the small farm enterprise, the mitigation of slavery and the reduction of the number of slaves, compensated for by the introduction and increase of services, were probably consequences rather than aims of this policy. In my opinion, its fundamental aim was an increase of production through an optimisation of efficiency. This production increase was in manual crafts as well as in agriculture with the aim of increasing deliveries of supplies to the church, the court and to the army. But did the latter need this increase?

How these deliveries were organised is well known only for abbeys and their estates. On supplies to the court and to the army only a few capitularies, among which the famous *Capitulare de villis*, give some scanty information. Of the production of royal fiscs one-third had to go to the court, one-third had to be consumed on the fisc itself, and one-third had to be stored awaiting further instructions or had to be sold. As for the army the provisions *ad hostem* (*hostilitium, carnaticum*), often replaced by payments in money, are regularly listed in the polyptychs of ecclesiastical estates as a burden on the free tenants. Besides monasteries and episcopal churches had to perform the *servitium regis*. Not only did contingents organised and supplied by churches form a significant part of Carolingian armies,[70] but frequently abbeys had to accommodate the king and his household. Therefore more supplies than needed by the abbey's population alone had to be transported to its seat. This was organised by transport services imposed on the producing manor's tenants and directed to intermediate regional centres from where the goods were brought by carts and ships or rafts to the abbey. The system is well documented in the polyptychs of St Germain-des-Prés, Prüm and St Remi of Reims.[71] From the

---

[70] Nelson, *Charles the Bald*, p. 58.

[71] Devroey, 'Services de transport'; Jean-Pierre Devroey, 'Un monastère dans l'économie d'échanges: les services de transport à l'abbaye de Saint-Germain-des-Prés au IXe siècle', *Annales. Economie–Sociétés–Civilisations* (1984), pp. 570–89, reprinted in Devroey, *Grand Domaine*.

so-called *Statutes* of abbot Adalhard of Corbie from 822, in which the abbot calculates the supply, mainly of grain, needed by the abbey's population, we learn that the distance of the grain producing manors to Corbie was taken into account to decide to sell the surplus of some distant manors on the spot instead of transporting it to the abbey.[72] St Germain-des-Prés on the other hand had all the wine from its wine-producing manors, and even wine the abbey had bought in regions where it had no possessions, brought to Paris. In this way it had a surplus to commercialise of 5,000 hectolitres which was probably sold at the fair of St Denis. The same must more or less have been true for the wine from the Moselle region produced by the manors of Prüm, although the evidence is less clear. Exports of wine from Prüm down and upstream the Moselle river to Worms, Cologne, Metz and Verdun seem to have been organised by the transport services of the abbey's tenants.

These activities, which are often difficult to characterise either as domanial or commercial, raise the general problem of the destination of the surplus of manorial production. Did the big abbeys organise their production deliberately to obtain a surplus and eventually to sell it? Was it out of necessity to have money to buy goods which they did not or could not produce, which was the only tolerated '*negocium*'? These are questions to which a possible answer can only be given in a more general evaluation of the aims and results of Carolingian economy.

[72] Adriaan Verhulst and Josef Semmler, 'Les statuts d'Adalhard de Corbie de l'an 822', *Le Moyen Age* 68 (1962), pp. 246–51.

4

AGRICULTURAL TECHNIQUE

In many areas between the Alps, the North Sea, the river Loire and the Rhine, a primitive irregular fallow system to restore fertility to the soil, in which the same crop was grown for several years in a row before the soil was left fallow for a similar length of time, had been superseded in the centuries before and at the beginning of the Middle Ages by a more regular fallow system with one grain crop and shorter, more regular, three-year periods of fallow. This system in turn evolved during the ninth century into a system in which two kinds of grain instead of one were grown in regular rotation side by side during the same harvesting year, namely winter-sown corn and spring-sown corn. Every third year the fields that had produced spring corn the year before were left lying fallow for a year, before being sown, after two ploughing turns in June and October, with winter corn, followed in the subsequent spring by the sowing of spring corn. This is what is called the three-course rotation, to be distinguished from the later topographical three-field system, in which three fields corresponded each to one of the phases just indicated. The new system made the cultivation of two different and complementary grain crops possible: one – spelt, rye and wheat – was meant for human consumption as grain for bread, while the other – mainly barley and oats – was used as animal feed. All these grains had the advantage of being sown and harvested at different times (autumn and spring) thus distributing field work more evenly and lessening the risk of a failed harvest. It was even possible in spring to sow a field with spring corn in those plots where the winter crop appeared to have failed. The proportion of fallow land was, furthermore, reduced from at least a half to a third, which led to a more intensive use of arable soil and a larger volume of production.

The origin of the three-course rotation has been the object of much discussion, especially among German scholars, who unnecessarily complicated the problem by making a connection between three-course rotation and the three-field system. One of them, Hildebrandt, thinks that a more primitive three-course rotation, in which spring corn dominated, was in place in the early Middle Ages and that an expansion of winter corn led to a more balanced three-course rotation.[1] His opinion was based on the Carolingian polyptych of Wissembourg abbey in Alsace,[2] but was rejected by Morimoto using the same document.[3] The latter, while admitting that in the oldest parts of the polyptych (*c.* 860) the rotation between different grain crops was less balanced, concluded that this meant that an evolution was going on towards a more regular three-course rotation through the introduction of more spring-grown crops. For him the basic crop at the start was winter corn and the expansion of spring corn during the ninth century made a more balanced three-course rotation possible. The polyptych of St Remi de Reims[4] strengthened him in this idea, for not only on the abbey's demesnes but also on the lands of the tenants, winter-grown crops originally dominated nearly exclusively. Other ninth-century polyptychs showed respectively progress of the three-course rotation between two chronological layers (868–9 and 889) as in the polyptych of the abbey of Lobbes and a more developed three-course system on the demesnes than on the tenants' plots at the abbey of Montiérender.[5] The latter observation raises the question of whether the new system was limited to demesnes or more collectively organised, to include holdings. One may even put the question whether the three-course rotation originated on demesne or tenants' lands. Although impossible to answer for the moment, the so-called 'lot-corvée', a plot of the demesne (called

---

[1] H. Hildebrandt, 'Systems of Agriculture in Central Europe up to the Tenth and Eleventh Centuries', in Della Hooke (ed.), *Anglo-Saxon Settlements* (Oxford, 1988), pp. 81–101.

[2] Dette (ed.), *Liber possessionum Wizenburgensis*.

[3] Yoshiki Morimoto, 'L'assolement triennal au haut Moyen Age. Une analyse des données des polyptyques carolingiens', in Verhulst and Morimoto (eds.), *L'économie rurale et L'économie urbaine*, pp. 91–125.

[4] Devroey (ed.), *Polyptyque de Saint-Remi de Reims*.

[5] Devroey (ed.), *Polyptyque Saint-Pierre de Lobbes*; Morimoto, 'Assolement triennal', p. 115.

ancinga in the polyptychs) regularly tilled by the same tenant for his lord, possibly has a key function in the resolution of this question. On evidence from the polyptychs of the abbeys of St Germain-des-Prés and St Remi de Reims, Morimoto noticed a more developed three-course rotation on parts of the demesne worked upon by the system of 'lot-corvée'.[6] He also noticed their topographical concentration in one part of the demesne and their lay-out in parallel long narrow strips in the same way as centuries later in the furlongs of a completed three-field system. Although dependent farmers thus knew the three-course rotation system, it is not certain that they were able to apply it themselves to their own land, even if they wanted to. The system implies that all plots cultivated according to it undergo the same kind of tillage at the same time and that once they have been sown they are not indiscriminately accessible to humans or animals. This is most easily achieved when all plots are located within the same field complex and are cultivated by and for the benefit of one owner, who is not obliged to take into account other farmers and neighbours. This was true for the larger complexes called *culturae*, of which the demesne of a large landowner usually consisted. The plots of individual farmers, however, with the exception of the 'lot-corvée', which in a way ended in being considered theirs, were usually well clear of the lands of the demesnes but were often intermingled with each other. This meant the three-course system could only be applied if all involved were in agreement. Even a clearly visible topographic division of arable land into three-field complexes can only have been applied (and not even generally at that) on the demesne lands in so far as they consisted of one or more of such complexes. This was not yet the case in all areas in the ninth century. Those scholars who presumed grouping in three units for those demesne lands that consisted of numerous complexes (*culturae*), even if their total number was a multiple of three, therefore, were wrong. The estate of Prüm in Mabompré in the Belgian Ardennes, for example, consisted of fifteen scattered *culturae*.[7] The terms *cultura*, *zelga*, *campus*, *satio*, *aratura*, *territorium*, used in many contemporary texts in connection with the three-course crop rotation system, should therefore not yet be interpreted as topographic-geographic subdivisions of arable land but merely as a reference to lands of the demesne sown with the same crop.[8] Thus the open field most probably did not yet exist. The field

---

[6] Morimoto, 'Assolement triennal', pp. 107–14.
[7] Schwab, *Prümer Urbar*, p. 208.
[8] Morimoto, 'Assolement triennal', pp. 93–4.

complexes – either demesne lands known as *culturae* or plots of individual farmers forming what was called an *accara* – did not yet form
continuous open areas and were still separated by woods, heath, or
uncultivated plots and possibly even enclosed by hedgerows or trees.
Only within the complexes did the plots probably together constitute
a kind of 'micro open field'.[9]

In spite of the importance of the sylvo-pastoral element in the
form of hunting, fishing or wild fruits in the early medieval economy
and food supply,[10] there is no doubt that grain production in the
Carolingian period made considerable progress and had become more
important than cattle raising or other forms of agrarian economy.
This was even the case in a country such as Italy, where a proportion
of half and half between wild and cultivated land in the triangle
Milan–Como–Varese was considered very high for arable land. It
was a higher proportion than the as yet little-exploited valley of the
Po with its numerous and extensive boglands.

The pollen diagrams and the increase in three-course crop ro-
tations, as seen from most polyptychs, prove this progress of grain
production. It was however unrelated to the yield ratios of the various grain crops, for which only very rare, unreliable and ambiguous
figures are available. It is now accepted that the very low yield ratios
that were calculated by Duby and Slicher van Bath[11] on the basis of
the inventory of grain stocks at the royal estates near Lille around
800 (mainly at Annappes), 1:3, 1:1.6, 1:1.3, 1:1.8, 1:2.15 for spelt,
wheat, rye, barley and oats respectively, should be increased slightly
in order to express real physical gross yields.[12] Although it is therefore no longer possible to refer to these yield ratios as catastrophic,
the expansion in the Carolingian period did not entail an increase
in efficiency but rather a production increase due to reclamations
and the adoption of the three-course crop rotation system. In itself
this important progress in agricultural technique did not lead to an
increase in physical efficiency.

[9] See Chapter 1.
[10] Massimo Montanari, *La faim et l'abondance. Histoire de l'alimentation en Europe*
(Paris, 1995), pp. 53–8.
[11] Georges Duby, 'Le problème des techniques agricoles', in *Agricoltura e mondo
rurale in Occidente nell'alto medioevo* (Spoleto, 1966), pp. 267–83; Bernard Slicher
van Bath, 'Le climat et les récoltes en haut moyen âge', in *Agricoltura e mondo rurale
in Occidente nell' alto medioevo*, pp. 399–425.
[12] Toubert, 'La part du grand domaine', pp. 73–4.

In south-west Germany, northern France and the southern half of present-day Belgium there was in the ninth century a very great prevalence of spelt.[13] It accounted for between 50 and 80 per cent of grain production. This crop, *triticum spelta* is related to *triticum aestivum*, which is wheat. As opposed to the latter, which is a 'naked' grain, spelt has a husk around the grain. This is favourable to its conservation and explains the large stocks of spelt, as opposed to the near absence of wheat, rye and oats, in inventories such as the *Brevium exempla*, which describe some royal estates around Lille at the beginning of the ninth century. Its disadvantage is its small yield, compensated for however, by a better resistance to climatic conditions. The difficult separation of the husk from the grain, which needs special mill stones or hand mills, is probably one of the reasons for the decline of spelt after the ninth century. On the other hand spelt is not very exigent concerning soil conditions and gives relatively good and regular yields on poor, light and chalky soils, such as those of the Champagne. The demesnes of St Remi de Reims in this region between the river Marne and the Ardennes, consisted mainly of immense *culturae* of several hundreds of hectares, where only spelt was grown. Against a demesne production consisting of 90 per cent of spelt, rents and income from mills, representative of peasant farms, consisted of 67 per cent of spelt. Its production of flour is 50 per cent, against 70 per cent from wheat.

The decline of spelt after the ninth century is also part of a more general progress of 'naked' grain during the tenth and eleventh centuries, especially of rye and wheat. Since the fourth century in north-east Germany the growth of rye had increased and it became more important than barley in central and western Gaul between the eighth and tenth centuries. It was grown on the small enclosed fields (*campi*) of a few hectares on the demesnes of St Remi de Reims. Wheat became important only from the tenth century onwards.

Oats were an expanding spring-sown grain in the early Middle Ages. Easily adaptable to poor soils, it was a pioneer plant for marginal and recently cleared land, especially up to the middle of the ninth century. For example, in the Belgian Ardennes on the estates of the

[13] Jean-Pierre Devroey, 'Entre Loire et Rhin: les fluctuations du terroir de l'épeautre au moyen âge', in J.-P. Devroey and J.-J. Van Mol (eds.), *L'épeautre (Triticum spelta), histoire et ethnologie* (Treignes, 1989), pp. 89–105, reprinted in Devroey, *Grand domaine*; Jean-Pierre Devroey, 'La céréaliculture dans le monde franc', in *L'ambiente vegetale nell'alto medioevo* (Spoleto, 1990: Settimane di studio 37), pp. 221–53, reprinted in Devroey, *Grand domaine*.

abbey of Prüm only oats were cultivated. From the second half of the ninth century onwards oats were more and more inserted as spring corn in the then expanding three-course rotation.

The expansion of the cultivation of summer grain, barley and oats within a three-course rotation enabled farmers to keep more cattle. Nevertheless, the raising of cattle was far less common than that of smaller domestic animals such as pigs or sheep, even on demesnes. The prevalence of pigs (on average 40 per cent of all domestic animals) in comparison to sheep and especially to cattle (22 per cent), on both demesne lands and farms held in tenure, points to mixed farming in which the stock economy was subordinate to an agricultural economy centred on grain production. This was true for both northern and southern Europe, which have been contrasted too strictly as a Germanic animal-fat economy as against a Roman olive and grain producing economy.[14] Yet, there were some regions in northern Europe in the eighth and ninth centuries where cattle raising was more important than agriculture. In Frisia the area of landownership of the abbey of Fulda was expressed in terms of the animals, cattle, sheep and pigs, that could be put to pasture on it.[15] Along the coasts of the Low Countries huge flocks of sheep were kept not only by nearby Flemish abbeys, like St Peter's and St Bavo's abbeys in Ghent, but also by abbeys farther away in Germany and France.[16] Their enormous wool production largely surpassed the need of the abbeys that possessed them. A pastoral specialisation of this kind does not point to an underdeveloped economy but, on the contrary, presupposes a specialised trade in and processing of wool, both in the country, mainly in Frisia, and in the developing towns of, for example, Flanders. The church in this respect, played an important role, for its widely scattered landholdings made it easier for it to run the risks associated with specialisation.

Cattle raising, however, did not solve the fundamental fertiliser problem, as long as it did not increase within the framework of a grain economy. In the ninth century only a modest step was taken in that direction. Agricultural technology remained too underdeveloped.

---

[14] Wickham, *Land and Power*, pp. 127–31.

[15] Stéphane Lebecq, *Marchands et navigateurs frisons du haut moyen âge*, 2 vols. (Lille, 1983), vol. I, pp. 126–8.

[16] W. Jappe Alberts and H. P. H. Jansen, *Welvaart in Wording. Sociaal-economische geschiedenis van Nederland van de vroegste tijden tot het einde van de Middeleeuwen* (The Hague, 1964), pp. 42–3.

The introduction of the heavy asymmetrical plough with mould board, for example, was an innovation that has been incorrectly placed in the eighth or ninth century.[17] In fact, archaeological evidence proves that it had been in use in various regions of western and central Europe as early as the second century, with its front train on two wheels. It is nevertheless possible that the distribution of the heavy plough was stimulated by the general economic expansion of the Carolingian period and by the use of iron. *Carruca* with the meaning 'plough', clearly pointing to the plough's front train, occurs for the first time in the famous polyptych of Irmino of St Germain-des-Prés from the 820s.[18] The labour services called *corvada* in the same polyptych are ploughing services to be executed by the tenants with their own plough and team of oxen. In the polyptych of the abbey of St Maur-des-Fossés *mansi carroperarii* are farms equipped with wheeled ploughs, as opposed to *mansi manoperarii* that had none. Not only in the latter abbey but also in several others like Wissembourg, St Germain-des-Prés and Fulda iron ploughshares had to be delivered, probably by specialised craftsmen or smiths, to the demesne. The scarcity of iron in the Carolingian period, alleged by Duby and others, is a myth, as will appear from Chapter 5. But equally incorrect is the famous thesis of Lynn White Jr[19] concerning the use of the horse as draught-animal thanks to the introduction of a fixed halter, the use of which in Roman times has since been proved.[20] Oxen continued, at least until the thirteenth century and even later, to be

---

[17] Axel Steensberg, 'Agrartechnik der Eisenzeit und des frühen Mittelalters', in Heinrich Beck, Dietrich Denecke and Herbert Jankuhn (eds.), *Untersuchungen zur eisenzeitlichen und frühmittelalterlichen Flur in Mitteleuropa und ihrer Nutzung*, 2 vols. (Göttingen, 1980: Abhandlungen der Akademie, Phil. -Histor. Klasse, III, no. 116), II, pp. 55–76; Dieter Hägermann and Helmuth Schneider, *Landbau und Handwerk 750 v. Chr. Bis 1000 n. Chr.* (Berlin, 1991: Propyläen Technikgeschichte), pp. 380–92; Georges Comet, 'Technology and Agricultural Expansion in the Middle Ages: The Example of France North of the Loire', in Grenville Astill and John Langdon (eds.), *Medieval Farming and Technology* (Leiden, 1997), pp. 21–4; Elmshäuser and Hedwig, *Studien Saint-Germain-des-Prés*, pp. 353–5.

[18] Hägermann and Schneider, *Landbau*, pp. 390–1; Elmshäuser and Hedwig, *Studien Saint-Germain-des-Prés*, p. 354, note 107.

[19] Lynn White Jr, *Medieval Technology and Social Change* (Oxford, 1962).

[20] Georges Raepsaet, 'The Development of Farming Implements between the Seine and the Rhine from the Second to the Twelfth Centuries', in Astill and Langdon (eds.), *Medieval Farming*, pp. 41–68; Hägermann and Schneider, *Landbau*, pp. 397–401.

the draught-animals *par excellence* for ploughing. The cultivation of
summer grain, barley and oats, within the three-course rotation, enabled farmers to keep more oxen still, at least four of which were
needed to pull a heavy plough.

In the Carolingian period the main technical equipment for the
working up of grain was the watermill (*molendinum*, *farinarium*).[21]
Although better represented in Antiquity than earlier scholars have
thought, the Carolingian period witnessed, as Marc Bloch once wrote
in a famous article, its triumph.[22] Evidently such a success has all to
do with the increase of grain production. Written evidence is, however, very unevenly distributed over the abbeys who were the main
originators and builders of the mills. There is no or only scanty information for most Italian abbeys (except S. Giulia of Brescia with
23 mills) nor for such big abbeys as St Denis or St Gall. Apart
from an inventory of St Wandrille abbey (787) listing 63 mills, most
quantitative information is to be found in the polyptychs of the
big Carolingian abbeys. Irmino's polyptych for St Germain-des-Prés
(*c.* 825) lists 84 mills (concentrated in 16 of 22 listed manors). The
other ninth-century polyptychs give the following figures: Prüm 45,
Wissembourg 12, St Bertin 13, Lobbes 29, St Remi de Reims 13,
Montiérender 18. The *Statutes* of Adalhard of Corbie (822), which
have an important section on the exploitation of mills,[23] mention
12 of them in the immediate neighbourhood of the abbey. These
absolute figures, when related to the arable land of the demesnes to
which these mills belong and to the number of peasant's farms, allow
the conclusion that the very great majority of peasants had access to
a mill in their own estate or at not too great a distance. If the number
of *villae* having a mill may seem low compared to the total number of
villae of an abbey, one has to take into account the natural, that is the
hydrographical conditions, the geographical situation (estates distant
from the seat of the abbey had less mills, except those of St Germain-
des-Prés in the rich grain producing regions of western France) and
the importance of arable land in the *villa* and its demesne, to which
the number of mills was clearly related.

---

[21] Etienne Champion, *Moulins et meuniers carolingiens dans les polyptyques entre Loire et
Rhin* (Paris, 1996); Hägermann and Schneider, *Landbau*, pp. 346–73.

[22] Marc Bloch, 'Avènement et conquêtes du moulin à eau', *Annales d'Histoire
Economique et Sociale* 7 (1935), pp. 538–63.

[23] Verhulst and Semmler, 'Statuts', pp. 241–6.

The standard type in the plains of north-west Europe, where watercourses have a normal flow and where the declivity is slight, was the vertical watermill, moved by the water under the wheel. Technically it may be supposed to have still been of the same type in the Carolingian period as the mill described by Vitruvius (33–22 BC). Most mills had several wheels, normally placed in parallel. The mills of Corbie, described by abbot Adalhard, had six wheels. In most cases dams and canals had to be built to guarantee a regular supply of the water. These were sometimes big works, as for example when Odland, abbot of St Bertin (798–805), deflected the upper course of the river Aa near St Omer over a distance of 2.5 km to build the mills at Arques.[24]

The building of a mill represented such an enormous investment of capital, that in the central regions of the Frankish empire they were usually in the ownership of a large ecclesiastical landowner as part of the demesne. Abbot Irmino of St Germain-des-Prés ordered himself the building of seven mills.[25] Normally mills were operated by tenants. They had to see that the income from the mill, which mostly consisted of grain and not flour, came into the hands of the abbey. In the manor of Villemeux, in the rich grain producing region between Dreux and Chartres, belonging to the abbey of St Germain-des-Prés, the income from 22 of the 28 mills on the rivers Eure and Blaise, amounted to 75,000 litres of grain, at an average rent of 5,000 litres per mill.[26] This total sum roughly equalled the needs of the abbey community, so that the income from all the other mills of St Germain could be brought to the market. The miller had a fairly autonomous position within the manor and, apart from paying the rent to the abbey, which he collected from the peasants who brought their grain to the mill, had no other significant obligations than those connected with the maintenance of the mill. The success of the watermill must certainly have caused the progressive disappearance of the handmill, which in turn continued the decline of the cultivation of spelt, the difficult husking and milling of which had needed hand work and could not be done by the big new watermill.

[24] Alain Derville, 'Le marais de Saint-Omer', *Revue du Nord* 62 (1980), pp. 73–95, reprinted in Alain Derville, *Douze études d'histoire rurale. Flandre, Artois, Cambrésis au moyen âge* (Lille, 1996), pp. 67–88, esp. p. 74.
[25] Elmshäuser and Hedwig, *Studien Saint-Germain-des-Prés*, pp. 436–65.
[26] *Ibid.*; Hägermann and Schneider, *Landbau*, pp. 368–70.

Wine-growing is a special branch of the agrarian economy and does not at all pose the same problems as grain cultivation.[27] It works with simple instruments and is in this, as in many other respects, the continuation of antique traditions. Only special knowledge of the treatment of vintage is required. In the Carolingian period the geographical distribution of wine-growing was the same as in Antiquity, spreading from Italy and southern France to the most northerly wine-producing regions around Paris and in the valleys of the rivers Moselle, Rhine and Main. In these northern regions more than in the south and Italy, wine-growing was part of the manorial organisation, more specifically of the exploitation of the demesne. The work was generally done the whole year through by unfree inhabitants of the manor. Unlike arable farming it was not bound to seasons, except for the vintage in autumn. Therefore, the system of 'lot-corvée', which was described earlier, was widely used as obligatory service. The same parcel of the vineyard, still as part of the demesne, was given for cultivation to the vintager, who by a natural evolution gradually came to consider it as his own. Already in Carolingian times some vintagers were allowed to hold their original 'lot-corvée'-parcel *ad medietatem*, that is in exchange for half the production. The situation on some estates was still more advantageous for them, as for example on the estate of the abbey of Prüm at Mehring, discussed below. Ordinary peasants in wine-growing regions had to deliver stakes for vines, and staves and hoops for casks. An estate of the abbey of Prüm had to deliver one cask and twelve hoops; a manor of St Germain-des-Prés 780 staves for 32 casks and the necessary hoops. Big casks with iron hoops had to be delivered to the army and the palace. The wine press on the demesne was the object of special care according to the *Capitulare de Villis*.[28] It might therefore be supposed to be a screw-press, although evidence for this type of press dates only from the tenth and eleventh centuries. Otherwise a simple beam was used levering big square wooden blocks.

[27] Hägermann and Schneider, *Landbau*, pp. 402–7; *Le vigneron, la viticulture et la vinification en Europe occidentale au moyen âge et à l'époque moderne* (Auch, 1991: Flaran 11); Elmshäuser and Hedwig, *Studien Saint-Germain-des-Prés*, pp. 365–99; M. Matheus (ed.), *Weinbau zwischen Maas und Rhein in der Antike und im Mittelalter* (Trierer Historische Forschungen 23, 1997).
[28] L. Clemens and M. Matheus, 'Zur Keltertechnik in karolingischer Zeit', in *Liber Amicorum für A. Heit* (1995), pp. 255–65.

Many abbeys had the wine from their vineyards transported by the obligatory services of their tenants. The system was particularly developed by the abbey of Prüm, on ships and even on rafts, down the Moselle.[29] It is generally accepted that the wine production of many abbeys exceeded their needs and that their surplus was conducted into commercial circuits. The abbey of Prüm received a total production of about 120,000 litres. One-fifth (24,000 litres) of it came from the village of Mehring on the Moselle, not far from the abbey, which was Prüm's most important wine-producing estate.[30] The total production of the eight Mehring vineyards (about 30 hectares), divided in 57 or 58 units of exploitation, called *pictura*, was however, 72,000 litres, three times that figure. Each tenant of such a *pictura*-parcel had to deliver 390 to 450 litres, which was indeed only a third of his production. Two-thirds could thus be sold by the tenants, who had to buy corn, meat and dung, stimulating in that way a money economy. There was one press at Mehring for which the landless unfree labourers (*hagastaldi*) of Prüm had to saw big square wooden blocks (Lat. *matrimen*) in the nearby Mehringer forest.

When seen against the clear and numerous signs of expansion of grain production, the famines of the eighth and ninth centuries are difficult to explain. It has been pointed out, possibly rightly, that they were less numerous in the two centuries before than after 1000, a fact which was considered to be related to the increased importance of grain in the diet after that date. It could also be said, however, that when we view these four centuries together, famine was more frequent in the ninth and in the twelfth centuries, that is, in the most expansive centuries at least as far as reclamations are concerned. This might lead to the conclusion that the famines in those centuries should not be interpreted primarily as a result of an underdeveloped agricultural economy, but rather as a consequence of too rapid an increase in population in comparison with the available means in terms of arable land or technology. They should perhaps, therefore, be seen as 'accidents' of expansion.

---

[29] Devroey, 'Services de transport à Prüm'.
[30] Franz Irsigler, 'Mehring. Ein Prümer Winzerdorf um 900', in Jean-Marie Duvosquel and Erik Thoen (eds.), *Peasants and Townsmen in Medieval Europe. Studia in Honorem Adriaan Verhulst* (Ghent, 1995), pp. 297–324.

5

CRAFT AND INDUSTRIAL PRODUCTION

—————— . ——————

As distinct from the situation in Merovingian times, when some of the artisanal and industrial activities dealt with hereafter took place mostly in an urban context, in Carolingian Europe textiles, tools, weapons and other iron and wooden objects, glass, pottery and salt were manufactured predominantly in a rural and manorial context. The best documented exception to this location is the artisanal quarter, sometimes arranged as a small town (*vicus*), annexed to or integrated in some big abbeys, like Corbie, St Riquier, St Gall or San Vincenzo al Volturno.[1] Manual workers with diverse specialities such as leather-working, metal-working smiths and weaponmakers, woodturners and other wood-workers and fur-makers had to provide for the needs of very large abbey communities. On the famous groundplan of St Gall abbey (*c.* 825–30),[2] a large workshop for various crafts is depicted together with a brewery, mills, an *officina* for fullers and other workshops. In St Riquier the settlement consisted of districts or streets (*vici*) where the artisans lived together grouped by speciality. Even though the artisans seem to have been more independent than the numerous unskilled *provendarii* that lived near the abbey as well, they did in fact belong to the unfree or half-free *familia* of the abbey. It is therefore questionable whether they worked for their own benefit. At San Vincenzo al Volturno, not far to the east of Monte

[1] Emile Lesne, *Histoire de la propriété ecclésiastique en France*, 6 vols. (Lille, 1943), vol. VI, pp. 391–424; Schwind, 'Zu karolingischen Klöstern als Wirtschaftsorganismen'.
[2] W. Horn and E. Born, *The Plan of St Gall*, 3 vols. (Berkeley, Los Angeles, London, 1979).

Cassino and on the border of Lombard and Beneventan territories, recent excavations by Richard Hodges[3] brought to light the existence during one generation, up to the 820s, of a builders' yard, where tiles for the basilica roof as well as the floors and roofs of other buildings were made. There then followed a phase in which the metal fittings of the monastery were made here. Finally the lamps and tableware were produced in a purpose-built workshop. The latter was demolished when the church was extended and a new collective workshop of the kind depicted on the St Gall plan was built. Traces of similar workshop complexes have been discovered in excavations of the monasteries at Augsburg and Corvey. The new workshops at San Vincenzo were producing luxury goods – commodities designed not only for use within the monastery, but also on its estates and within the households of its benefactors. Only four have so far been excavated. Enamels, cavalry equipment and glass-ware were made here. Pottery, leather goods, everyday metal equipment as well as ivories and bonework must have been made in other workshops.

Both archaeological and written evidence, most from estate inventories, prove that in the Carolingian period textile production was a normal side-activity of peasants' wives, except for the combing of raw wool and the fulling of the woven cloth, which was a men's activity.[4] On many manors deliveries had to be made by peasant households of woven pieces of linen cloth (*cam(i)siles, drappi*), of wool or of flax (*sar(i)ciles*), in both cases for the manufacturing of shirts (*camisiae*), or the shirts themselves had to be supplied in addition to coats and capes made of wool (*pallia, saga*). Sometimes spindles of spun flax (*fusa lini, ladmen*) had to be delivered, in quantities varying according to the free or unfree status of the women. This was the case for example, on the manor of Quelmes (ar. St Omer, cant. Lumbres), belonging to the abbey of St Bertin in north-west France around the middle of the ninth century,[5] on the manor of Villance in the Belgian Ardennes (prov. Luxembourg, ar. Neufchâteau, cant. St Hubert), belonging to the abbey of Prüm at the end of the ninth century[6] and particularly on many manors of the abbey of Lobbes in the Belgian province of Hainaut, described in an inventory of 868–9. On one of

---

[3] Richard Hodges, *Light in the Dark Ages. The Rise and Fall of San Vincenzo al Volturno* (London, 1997).

[4] Hägermann and Schneider, *Landbau und Handwerk*, pp. 479–91.

[5] Ganshof, *Polyptyque Saint-Bertin*, pp. 32–3.

[6] Schwab, *Prümer Urbar*, pp. 201–8.

its manors 1925 spindles (*fusa*) had to be delivered, on another 1000, and elsewhere from 15 to 1200.[7] The cultivation of flax must have been widespread in southern Belgium and northern France during the ninth century. It was perhaps made possible by the extension of arable land on the occasion of the introduction of the three-course rotation system. Sometimes services of textile working or deliveries of wool or flax were redeemable as was the case, on a temporary basis, i.e. as long as the manor was given out in *beneficium* to a certain Salaco, on the manor of St Amand's abbey at Maire, near the city of Tournai. According to the fragment of a ninth-century (821–72) inventory of the manors given out *in beneficium*,[8] six households (*mansi*) each paid two pennies every third year instead of the delivery of wool (*pro lana*) and four of them one penny instead of spinning (*pro filatura*). Six female shirt-makers (*camsilariae*), each perhaps living on one of the six *mansi*, redeemed the making of cloth for shirts (*camsiles*) by paying eight pennies. It would be difficult to imagine that during the time the manor was not directly in the hands of the abbey, they stayed unemployed. These women probably went on spinning and weaving and sold their production in the nearby city of Tournai, which already at that time, continuing a Roman tradition, must have been famous for its cloth. When the manor in 872 returned to the abbey the six *mansi* at Maire were working for the clothing service (*ad vestimentorum usus*) of the abbey.[9]

The six female shirt-makers at Maire near Tournai seem to have enjoyed a fair degree of liberty. This was not the case in the workplaces for women (*gynaecea*) that are mentioned from the eighth century onward in various places in Europe. Both female slaves without a holding of their own and half-free women with holdings, often of servile status (*mansus servilis*), had to come and work there as an obligatory service that more or less corresponded to the agricultural seigneurial services of the men on the demesnes. The *gynaeceum* was normally part of a manor's demesne and situated not far from it. On royal estates it was organised as a separate quarter, closed with hedges and a gate. We do not know, however, if it consisted of one great building with rooms where the unfree women lived permanently or if it was also composed of several so-called 'sunken huts'

---

[7] Devroey (ed.), *Polyptyque Lobbes*, pp. 5–17.

[8] Hägermann and Hedwig (eds.), *Polyptychon Saint-Maur-des-Fossés*, pp. 88, 104.

[9] Henri Platelle, *Le temporel de l'abbaye de Saint-Amand des origines à 1340* (Paris, 1962), p. 80 n. 41 and p. 100.

(Germ. *Grubenhäuser*). These were small workshops of only a few square metres (2.7 m – 2.5 m) and suited for one, two or three persons, dug out in the ground at half a metre to one metre, where loom weights have been found that had stretched the warp-threads of a vertical and not very broad (1.25 m) weaving loom, such as the one depicted in the famous Utrecht psalter (817–34).[10] Sunken huts of the ninth century have been excavated near the main farm building of a demesne and of individual holdings on some manors of the abbey of St Denis in the Paris region.[11] Many abbeys had a *gynaeceum* next to them or on one of their manors, where several tens of women worked: twenty-four at the small Bavarian abbey of Staffelsee, forty at Murbach abbey in Alsace, fifty-five at a manor of Fulda.[12] Weaving, however, as a typical female activity in those times, was never done in the abbey itself. Only a fuller's workshop is spotted on the St Gall cloisterplan and mentioned by Adalhard of Corbie in his *Statutes* as part of the abbey buildings. In the *Capitulare de Villis* and the *Brevium exempla gynaecea* are also mentioned, which means that they were common on royal domains (*fisci*).

Their production may be qualified industrial, that is to say quantitatively important but also qualitatively of high standard, which seems normal for specialised workers – as the women in the *gynaecea* must have been. This raises the much and still debated problem of the *pallia fresonica*, woollen cloth of a high quality that was renowned throughout the whole of the Frankish empire. As a diplomatic gift they were even offered by Charlemagne to Harun ar-Rashid, the caliph of Baghdad. As suggested by their name they should have been manufactured in Frisia, although some scholars have defended the idea that their transport alone was done by Frisians and that they were manufactured in England or in Flanders. The French historian Lebecq, specialist of the economic history of the North Sea regions and particularly of medieval Frisia, has since brought together all the arguments, written and archaeological, in favour of a Frisian origin of this cloth.[13] His strongest argument in my opinion is the archaeological discovery, both on the artificial mounds (known as *terpen*) in Frisia and in the Scandinavian sites of Hedeby and Birka (where

[10] Jean Chapelot and Robert Fossier, *Le village et la maison au moyen âge* (Paris, 1980), pp. 116–33.
[11] Cuisenier and Guadagnin (eds.), *Un village au temps de Charlemagne*, p. 279.
[12] Hägermann and Schneider, *Landbau und Handwerk*, pp. 486–90.
[13] Lebecq, *Marchands et navigateurs frisons*, vol. I, pp. 131–4.

Frisian merchants were active in the ninth century), of cloth of the same high quality besides ordinary cloth. The latter must have been the one delivered by Frisian peasants to the abbey of Fulda in huge quantities. An inventory of the Fulda possessions in Frisia *c.* 830 lists a total of 855 *pallia* to be delivered by about ten persons who held land there from the abbey.[14] Other abbeys too, located far away from the saltmarshes along the Flemish, Zeeland and Frisian coasts, like the Normandian abbey of St Wandrille or the abbey of Lorsch in Germany, brought in their wool from flocks of sheep that they owned there themselves, or took delivery of large annual supplies of woollen monks' clothes and other woven materials. It is not always clear, in cases when only pieces of cloth were delivered, where and by whom garments, frocks and other habits were made of them. That some abbeys bought them is not the only reason for us to think that there was an important market for textiles in the ninth century, not only of high quality or luxury goods.

Iron-working differentiated in two forms of production: the winning of iron ore and its transformation; the hammering and beating for the fabrication of arms, utensils and agricultural instruments.[15]

Archaeological excavations have uncovered 'mines' or surface furrows, pits and funnel shafts, dated between the eighth and tenth centuries, from which iron ore was extracted. These were often donated with the surrounding land by smaller private landowners to abbeys such as Fulda, Lorsch and St Gall. Only one written reference to an individual miner (*fossarius*) is known, namely on the lands of the abbey of Prüm in Houmont in the Belgian Ardennes.[16] Whether the *fossa ferraricia sive plumbaricia*, shallow shafts of iron ore and lead that are mentioned in the *Capitulare de Villis* (c. 62) as elements of the royal estate, were indeed mainly to be found on *fisci* is unclear, even though the only proof for the existence of industrial iron-working concerns possessions of the Carolingian king.

---

[14] *Ibid.*, vol. II, pp. 382–3.

[15] Rolf Sprandel, *Das Eisengewerbe im Mittelalter* (Stuttgart, 1968); Walter Janssen, 'Gewerbliche Produktion des Mittelalters als Wirtschaftsfaktor im ländlichen Raum', in Herbert Jankuhn, Walter Janssen, Ruth Schmidt-Wiegand and Heinrich Tiefenbach (eds.), *Das Handwerk in vor- und frühgeschichtlicher Zeit*, 2 vols. (Göttingen, 1983: Abhandlungen der Akademie der Wissenschaften, Phil. Histor. Klasse III, nos. 122–3), vol. II, pp. 331–47; Hägermann and Schneider, *Landbau und Handwerk*, pp. 419–34.

[16] Schwab, *Prümer Urbar*, p. 206.

In Germany, and the same must be true elsewhere, many installations for iron smelting start in the Carolingian period, often in combination with 'sunken huts' and of family type. Nearly in every Carolingian rural settlement iron-slags have been found, but archaeology cannot make clear if iron-working was a secondary activity of peasants or a primary activity of specialised craftsmen.It is likely that the rather small and strongly decentralised production of iron was processed locally by smiths. Written sources show the latter in different contexts: as tenant in a bipartite manor, paying rent but producing independently, or working for the lord's demesne as part of it, or as a free man working like the miller as a 'public service', accessible to everybody. There is archaeological evidence of the activity of smiths between 600 and 900 from the region of the upper Rhine (Schaffhausen) and the lower Rhine (Krefeld), from a mound in the Wesermarsh, in the Carolingian lost village under the Kootwijk-erzand and in other places on the Veluwe (Holland) and especially in the village of Warendorf (Westphalia). Here, not only were large parts of smelting furnaces found, but it was also possible to locate the workplace of a smith, which led to the conclusion that there was always one smith present per group of farms. It has been deduced from this evidence that these blacksmiths were probably integrated in the manorial structures. Specialised smiths are mentioned in Italian cities like Brescia, in abbeys like Corbie or in St Gall, where they forged swords. In the well-known inventory of the estates of the bishopric of Chur,[17] the income of a complete *ministerium* from the vicinity of Bregenz in the Vorarlberg consisted mainly of supplies of iron products paid as *census regis* to the representative of the king. Eight furnaces are mentioned. This substantial production clearly exceeded local needs and can therefore be termed 'industrial'. Almost all other written documents from such abbeys as Bobbio, St Remi de Reims, Wissembourg, Lorsch and St Gall record deliveries of iron, either as rough ingots (referred to by weight) or as finished products such as ploughshares, horseshoes and weapons, which served as rents from peasants for their holdings. The abbey of St Germain-des-Prés received 100 *librae de ferro* from each of its 25.5 *mansi serviles* in the *villa* of Boissy-Maugis in the Perche (western France).[18] This may

---

[17] Otto P. Clavadetscher, 'Zum churrätischen Reichsguturbar aus der Karolingerzeit', *Zeitschrift für schweizerische Geschichte* 30 (1950), pp. 161–97.
[18] Elmshäuser and Hedwig, *Studien Saint-Germain-des-Prés*, pp. 196–201.

indicate a community of iron smelters that lived somewhat isolated in one of the numerous extensive forests of this region. From thirteen tenants in Altenstadt the abbey of Wissembourg received sickles, axes and ploughshares, in exchange for a workshop (*fabrica*).[19] The abbey of Fulda received from its manor in Kissingen four iron cooking pots and the iron elements for two ploughs (*ferramenta semper ibi ad duo dantur aratra*). Kissingen consisted mainly of demesne land and had only four whole and five half-*mansi*, which were more engaged in artisanal than in agricultural activity. The demesne farm also claimed the yearly maintenance of a great number of agricultural instruments and utensils, such as sickles, axes, spades, etc. (*Falces minores X, maiores II, secures III, dolatoria II, patelle II, caldaria II. Hec omnia utensilia . . . sibi debet habere curia illa ad usus fratrum nostrorum et singulis annis reparari in melius*).[20] Similarly the tenants of the abbey of S. Giulia in Brescia had to deliver ploughshares, axes, saws, and more particularly pigs of iron, expressed in weights, several hundreds of pounds and bars of iron for sale.[21]

All these examples, which could be extended, contradict George Duby's and Robert Fossier's pessimistic interpretation of an inventory of agricultural instruments in the *Brevium exempla*. According to them,[22] the only six iron instruments recorded for the whole royal estate of Annappes, compared to the 'sufficient' number of wooden instruments (*ustensilia lignea ad ministrandum sufficienter*), reveal the poverty of Carolingian agriculture and economy.

That the Carolingian period witnessed a growing production of arms is not surprising in the light of the many examples of expanding iron production and against the background of the numerous wars and military expeditions by Charlemagne, particularly during the first decades of his reign. Several abbeys had arms manufactured for the military service of their vassals, and only for them. Selling them to other persons, particularly to merchants, was repeatedly forbidden.[23] Workshops for weapons are depicted on the St Gall cloister plan and mentioned at Bobbio, Corbie and other abbeys, often together with workshops for artisans for the working of leather, which was an

---

[19] Dette, *Liber Possessionum*, p. 105.
[20] Weidinger, 'Untersuchungen zur Grundherrschaft Fulda', pp. 255–6.
[21] Hägermann and Schneider, *Landbau und Handwerk*, pp. 433–4.
[22] Georges Duby, *L'économie rurale et la vie des campagnes dans l'Occident médiéval* (Paris, 1962), p. 77; Chapelot and Fossier, *Le village et la maison*, p. 24.
[23] Ganshof, *Frankish Institutions*, p. 66 and note 54 (on p. 159).

important element of the military equipment. The abbeys of Lorsch, St Gall and Fulda produced swords, increasingly damascened, the polishing and sharpening of the damascened blade being represented on one of the sketches of the Utrecht psalter.[24] From its manor at Boissy (in the Perche region, western France), already mentioned above for its iron production, the abbey of St Germain-des-Prés received six lances from one blacksmith for half a *mansus* (*Ermenulfus faber medietatem mansi de VI. lanceis*, Pol. Irm. XIII, 103),[25] besides 100 lb *de ferro* from half a *mansus servilis* and the same from most of the other *mansi serviles* there (Pol. Irm. XIII, 64, 66).[26] There is no doubt that on the royal estates the *ministeriales ferrarii*, which the *Capitulare de Villis* ordered careful registration of, made weapons besides agricultural instruments.

Carolingian pottery production is almost exlusively known from archaeological evidence. Unlike textile or iron production there is hardly any mention of ceramics in the many polyptychs of the Carolingian period. The reason may be that their production was no longer, as had been mostly the case in Merovingian times, a decentralised home activity and that pottery could now easily be purchased from some important production centres. Their sites were also different from Merovingian antecedents, which had often been located in towns. For the first time in the Middle Ages a qualitatively high mass production in the countryside was possible because it was organised in a manorial context.[27] Formal and stylistic features of ceramics allow better determination of the place and date of fabrication than for iron or glass, and thus aid identification. There is, however, one major difficulty as similarities lead to the conclusion that the same type was possibly made in different places, both because of links between them and through imitation. The best way forward, therefore, is the archaeological study of the place of fabrication itself.

The best studied areas of production within the Carolingian empire are the regions of the middle and lower Rhine downstream of Koblenz. The village of Badorf, between Bonn and Cologne, gave its name to a type of ceramics characteristic for the Carolingian period, but also present in different neighbouring villages, such as Walberberg and Eckdorf. An area of about 20 km formed a long

---

[24] Hägermann and Schneider, *Landbau und Handwerk*, p. 425.
[25] Hägermann (ed.), *Polyptychon Saint-Germain-des-Prés*, p. 117.
[26] *Ibid.*, pp. 112–13.
[27] Janssen, 'Gewerbliche Produktion', pp. 348–85.

coherent production chain, primarily determined by the presence of the necessary clay and sand, by the proximity of sources of energy such as water and wood, and also by the presence at a short distance of towns like Cologne or Andernach, functioning as export places. In Eckdorf seven ovens from the Carolingian period have been excavated. Another important Carolingian pottery centre was situated in Saran, in the forest of Orléans, but, unlike Badorf, outside the neighbouring settlement. The quality of the production in terms of the material, the shape, the decorations and the standardisation, and the sheer quantity apparent from the massive exports, clearly point to the industrial nature of Badorf and Saran. That the quality and quantity of pots produced in the Carolingian period was greater than that of the Merovingian period points to better organisation, probably within the manorial framework. Reference is made in this respect (without however written confirmation) to the spatial connections with the later possessions of the archbishop of Cologne and the chapter of St Pantaleon of Cologne in the vicinity of Badorf. Next to the king, these church institutions are considered possible patrons of the specialised craftsmen, who are believed, rightly or wrongly, to have had no independent status at all.

In Carolingian times salt-making took mainly three forms: evaporation through natural climatic factors of sea-water collected in man-made salt-gardens along the Atlantic coast of France and the Mediterranean; exploitation of salt-wells in many parts of central Europe; extraction of salt from peat by cooking.[28] The latter method was probably practised by different abbeys such as that of Lorsch in 776 on one of the Zeeland islands in the estuary of the Scheldt. In that year a certain Godebert bestowed on the abbey, a church, a *mansus*, the ground belonging to it, an unfree man with his wife and son and seventeen saltpans (*XVII culinas ad sal faciendum*).[29] This impressive number not only may be interpreted as an indication of an industrial exploitation but also of the importance of Zeeland, already at this early date, for salt production, which would be one of its major industries during the whole Middle Ages. Other abbeys too must have obtained salt from their Zeeland possessions, notwithstanding their remote situation. This was not only the case with Lorsch but also with the abbey of Nivelles, south of Brussels, which in 877 was

---

[28] Hägermann and Schneider, *Landbau und Handwerk*, pp. 408–18.
[29] Cornelis Dekker, *Zuid-Beveland. De historische geografie en de instellingen van een Zeeuws eiland in de Middeleeuwen* (Assen, 1971), p. 34.

confirmed by Charles the Bald the possession 'in Frisia' (that is the greater Frisia of the early Middle Ages, including Zeeland) of several tenants and their holdings, *ad salem*, i.e. for the abbey's supply with salt.[30]

The salt produced by the salt-gardens along the coast, mainly north and south of the estuary of the Loire, particularly in the Baie de Bourgneuf, was the object of a lively trade by many abbeys.[31] However, having no part in the exploitation of the salines, they were yet exempt from tolls on the Loire where some, like the abbey of St Mesmin of Micy at Port-Saint-Père, near the estuary of the Loire, possessed a landing-stage for the ships bringing in the salt from the Baie de Bourgneuf. The exploitation of the salines and perhaps also of the ships was probably in the hands of private and free entrepreneurs under supervision of the king. It was these men who in 821 were summoned to the emperor's court for account, in order to proceed to a fair settlement of a dispute that we know nothing further about:

De terra in litore maris ubi salem faciunt, volumus ut aliqui ex eis veniant ad placitum nostrum et ratio eorum audiatur, ut tunc secundum aequitatem inter eos definire valeamus, instruction of Louis the Pious to his *missi*; translation: concerning the land at the coast where they make salt, we want that some of them come to our court session and that their account be audited to enable us to settle the dispute between them with equity.[32]

There were also salt basins in some places on the northern coast of the Mediterranean. In the estuary of the Rhône salines were exploited on the shore of some *étangs*. In the lagoons of Venice and at the estuary of the Po (in Comacchio) the salt production was so important that it led in the ninth century to a wide network of inter-regional trade upstream along the Po. Salt-wells were quite numerous in central Europe and in Lotharingia. Technically they were exploited by conducting water into the wells, to obtain a liquid salt solution (Fr. *sole*) that was brought to the saline through wooden conduit-pipes. There the salt was crystallised in large cooking pots by means of boiling the water, which evaporated. Documents concerning salt production on the estates in Lorraine of the abbey of Prüm, not far from Metz in

---

[30] *Ibid.*

[31] François-L. Ganshof, 'A propos du tonlieu à l'époque carolingienne', in *La città nell'alto medioevo* (Spoleto, 1959: Settimane di studi del Centro italiano di studi sull'alto medioevo, 6), pp. 487–9.

[32] Boretius (ed.), *Capitularia*, I, no. 148, c.8.

Vic-sur-Seille, Moyenvic and Marsal provide some notion of industrial organisation.[33] Other abbeys with an eye to their need for salt,
such as those of St Denis, Montiérender and Wissembourg, also
had estates in this region. In Prüm's case, the sources of salt and the
collecting basins and workplaces with pots were all owned by the
abbey. The manual workers (*operatores*) were Prüm's tenants working
in exchange for holdings where they could also grow crops. They
could use the collecting basins and other utensils in exchange for
the payment of a tax that was calculated per boiling pot. They were
allowed to keep three parts of the production for sale, one part going
to the abbey, which had it transported by means of transport services
of tenants via Metz along the Moselle to the main seat of the abbey
in Prüm. The salt that was not used in the abbey itself was sold on
the local markets in the vicinity of Prüm. The exploitation of salt
from Prüm's estates in Lorraine, one may conclude, was organised
in a manorial context, but with a large autonomy for the artisans,
comparable to the position of smiths and millers.

The same can generally be said about the organisation of the salt
production from similar wells in central Europe of which those in Bad
Reichenhall in Bavaria were the most important. Already from the
eighth century onwards the Agilolfinger dukes of Bavaria had given
parts in these wells to abbeys in their duchy, such as Niederaltaich,
Mondsee and Tegernsee. Salt-wells were also the property of churches
in central Germany: in 823 the abbey of Fulda received their part in
the salt wells at Bad Kissingen from several free persons. Four salines
were exploited by the tenants of four *mansi* that probably had only this
artisanal and no agricultural function. They were moreover the only
holdings within this manor that at that moment consisted exclusively
of demesne land.[34]

The quality and quantity of glass production, especially as measured against its export in the Carolingian period to faraway regions
such as Scandinavia via Dorestad to Hedeby and Birka, allow us to
surmise that the production was on an industrial scale.[35] The only
two written references, however, in each case to a glazier who is
specifically named (*vitrearius*) as holder of a *mansus* and half a *mansus*
in the vicinity of Douai (northern France) and in Barisis (dép. Aisne)
on possessions of the abbey of St Amand in 864, are difficult to fit

[33] Kuchenbuch, *Bäuerliche Gesellschaft Prüm*, pp. 293–8.
[34] Weidinger, 'Untersuchungen zur Grundherrschaft Fulda', p. 255.
[35] Janssen, 'Gewerbliche Produktion', pp. 320–31.

in an industrial context.[36] It seems probable that these glaziers were, with other specialised artisans, normally active in the buildings of St Amand abbey and of its *cella* in Barisis. Apart from a glass-making workshop in the Carolingian palace at Paderborn, there is archaeological evidence concerning a glassmaker's workshop in the builders' yard of the abbey of San Vincenzo al Volturno, which is one of the outstanding discoveries of the excavations at this abbey by Richard Hodges.[37] It followed, in a dynamic process of successive workshops, a metal-working workshop. The glassmaker's workshop was a well-made building. The artisan was an exceptional craftsman, making wafer-thin vessels in opaque, pale blue and very pale green glass, many of which were decorated with trailing white or yellow lines. His output consisted primarily of bowls, dishes and lamps which constituted by far the bulk of his output. The glassmaker may also have been responsible for making the monastery's window panes. In the 820s, when work was set to begin on the eastwork in front of the main abbey church, the glass workshop was systematically demolished and a concrete mixer was set up close by as the foundations for a new workshop building were made.

Apart from these examples of glass production in abbeys, industrial glass production in the Carolingian period, unlike the Merovingian glasswork, was no longer situated in an urban context, but rather isolated in densely wooded areas, near the find-spot of raw materials such as wood, chalk, quartzs and and potash. Although there is only one case of archaeological evidence in the region, Carolingian glass production is mostly situated between the Meuse and the Rhine and particularly in the Argonne forest. The only excavated place of Carolingian glass manufacturing is located in the wooded region called Hochwald near Kordel, not far from Trier, where glassovens were found the funnelled cups of which, represented in the Utrecht psalter, were exported to Hedeby and Birka. It seems that the artisans did not live near the glass ovens but in settlements not far away.[38]

The conclusion of this chapter is that there was a very wide range of artisanal structures: from the secondary activity of peasants to the highly specialised and even artistic work of an individual artisan.

---

[36] François-L. Ganshof, 'Das Fränkische Reich', in Hermann Kellenbenz (ed.), *Handbuch der europäischen Wirtschafts- und Sozialgeschichte*, 6 vols. (Stuttgart, 1980), vol. II, p. 184 and p. 188 note 27.

[37] Hodges, *San Vincenzo al Volturno*, pp. 98–100 and *passim*.

[38] Janssen, 'Gewerbliche Produktion', pp. 323–5.

In economically autarchic regions the making of every-day objects, very often made of wood, the most common raw material, and also of bone, was generally a secondary activity of peasants. Tenants were often obliged to deliver to their lord wooden objects such as eating plates, spoons, roof shingles, slats, torches, vats, barrels and even carts. In polyptychs of big abbeys such as Prüm, St Bertin, Montiérender, St Maur-des-Fossés, Lobbes and even of smaller abbeys like St Peter's at Ghent, one can find numerous examples of manors in which such deliveries were a normal practice.

Primary artisanal activities were only possible either in industrial contexts, which were rare but not absent, for example in iron-working, salt-making and pottery, or in abbeys, royal courts and big estates and in beginning cities such as the *emporium* Dorestad. The *Capitulare de Villis*, *c.* 45, gives a long enumeration of craftsmen who were expected to be present on royal estates. The highest specialisation was possible at the royal court or in some abbeys, where some artisans became real artists, although their anonymity was the rule. The inscription 'ULFBERTH' on the blade of some highly priced swords is an exception. Professional free artisans living from their craft activity must equally have been exceptional, although wandering artisans, whose existence has been proved archaeologically, probably belonged to that category.

PART III

COMMERCE

6

ORGANISATION

———— • ————

Concerning commerce and trade one must be careful not to transpose in a simple way concepts and realities of today to the early Middle Ages. Commerce today means profit but not always in those centuries were goods sold and bought out of such motives. Buying and selling were often done out of necessity, not by professional merchants but by the producers and consumers themselves. In those cases money could be replaced by goods, as when for example abbot Adalhard of Corbie in his instructions (*Statuta*) for the economy of the abbey household from the year 822 ordered that the production surplus of its gardens should be sold either for money or for grain (*venundetur aut contra denarios aut contra annonam*).[1] Simple exchange without money also took place on a certain social level either as gifts of valuables between kings, princes and members of the aristocracy on some occasions, but also for more ordinary goods, such as lead or salt, for example between abbots when their abbey was in need of them and could not obtain them by purchase for some reason (e.g. scarcity).[2] Such transactions were sometimes considered as commercial by local agents and unjustly subjected to tolls. Tolls in principle were indeed levied only on commercial goods. Some historians even propose for the Carolingian

[1] Verhulst and Semmler, 'Statuts', p. 248.
[2] Philip Grierson, 'Commerce in the Dark Ages: a Critique of the Evidence', *Transactions of the Royal Historical Society*, 5th Series 9 (1959), pp. 123–40, reprinted in Philip Grierson, *Dark Age Numismatics* (London, 1979); John Moreland, 'Concepts of the Early Medieval Economy', in Hansen and Wickham (eds.), *The Long Eighth Century*, pp. 1–34, esp. pp. 5–8 ('Grierson and the Gift').

economy the model of a double circulation circuit:[3] a privileged one of producers and consumers buying and selling out of necessity and not for profit, through agents at their service, and a superimposed circuit of free professional merchants working for profit by means of money only and subjected to tolls.

However, in both cases and notwithstanding the alternative examples quoted above, money was normally needed as intermediary, even in a largely self-sufficient economy. Kings, princes, members of the aristocracy and dignitaries of the church, apart from their income by gifts, deliveries of dependants, tribute and plunder, needed money to buy rare commodities: overseas spices, jewels, silk and other costly textiles, weapons and in general goods that could not be obtained by trucking. Dependent peasants, although mostly bound to obligatory deliveries and services, had to pay some rents in cash, maybe by substitution, for example for military service (*hostilitium*). From time to time they had to buy seed and agricultural instruments from outside their farm. There is broad evidence for money circulation in the Carolingian period: texts concerning the payment, often in cash, of high tributes to Viking bands, texts concerning price regulations, archaeologically discovered hoards, etc. prove the use of money, available in large quantities since the introduction by Pipin III in 755 of a new silver penny (*denarius*), better adapted to daily commercial operations than the golden *tremissis* of the Merovingian period.[4]

As has been said a distinction must be made between on the one hand professional, free merchants (*mercatores*), some of them, like the Jews, protected and privileged by the king, and at the same time, beside their own professional activities, at his service, and on the other hand mere agents (*missi*) of churches and even of individuals. Through their commercial activity for the latter's account and sometimes because of their name (*neguciantes*), they are often difficult to differentiate from free merchants.[5] Indeed, they could change their

---

[3] Toubert, 'Part du grand domaine', pp. 85–6; Jean-Pierre Devroey, 'Courants et réseaux d'échange dans l'économie franque entre Loire et Rhin', in *Mercati e mercanti nell'alto medioevo* (Spoleto, 1993: Settimane di studio del Centro Italiano di studi sull'alto medioevo 40), pp. 378–9.

[4] See Part IV.

[5] Peter Johanck, 'Der fränkische Handel der Karolingerzeit im Spiegel der Schriftquellen', in Klaus Düwel, Herbert Jankuhn, Harald Siems, Dieter Timpe (eds.), *Untersuchungen zu Handel und Verkehr der vor- und frühgeschichtlichen Zeit in Mittel- und Nord-Europa*, 6 vols., vol. IV, *Der Handel der Karolinger- und Wikingerzeit* (Göttingen, 1987: Abhandlungen der Akademie der Wissenschaften, Phil.-Hist. Klasse, 3rd series, no. 156), pp. 55–60.

status, like a man called Ibbo who at the end of the eighth century
gave himself to the abbey of St Maximin at Trier after having been
a free merchant on his own.[6]

Other categories of merchants can be distinguished by their specialisation, such as slave-traders, wine merchants, tradesmen dealing
in salt, grain, etc. Wandering artisans selling their products, such as
glass, jewels and combs, also form a distinctive category. But specialisation is not always required, as is demonstrated by the fact that simple
dependants of an abbey, for example some tenants of the abbey of
Prüm, or estate officials of a higher rank, such as *maiores* or *villici*,
could be obliged to sell whatever they produced. Simple dependent
peasants were on the other hand allowed, after having paid their rents
and other duties to their lord, to sell the surplus of their production
at a price freely agreed between them and the buyer. The fact that
this was expressly stated by a church council in Paris in 829[7] shows
that some lords did not respect this freedom of retail trade. Finally,
some ethnic groups, not only Jews, but in the ninth century especially
Frisians,[8] and also foreigners from outside the Carolingian empire,
were more involved in commerce than others because of their mobility. Foreigners enjoyed special royal protection within the empire
by conventions of reciprocity negotiated on the diplomatic level, as
between Charlemagne and King Offa of Mercia in 796 and between
Louis the German and the Danish king in 873.[9]

Inside the Carolingian empire trade was carried on either on
so-called 'legitimate' or public markets (*mercatus legitimus, mercatus
publicus*), or on private markets, the latter mostly established within
a rural manor (*villa*, hence: *villa*-markets). A market toll was levied,
by the king, counts, churches and private lords respectively, which
authorised access to the market for merchants and the right to proceed
there to commercial operations between them.[10] Public toll places
were mostly situated in towns (*civitates, castella, portus, vicus*), but also in
ports, on river banks, or near ferries, bridges and fords, and of course
within royal manors. How tolls were levied on groups of merchants,
who are reported following the army to sell weapons, is not known.

[6] *Ibid.*, p. 62; Lebecq, *Marchands frisons*, pp. 28–9.
[7] Dopsch, *Wirtschaftentwicklung*, vol. II, p. 232 note 4.
[8] Lebecq, *Marchands frisons*, pp. 23–34.
[9] François-L. Ganshof, 'L'étranger dans la monarchie franque', in *Recueils Société
Jean Bodin* 10 (1958), pp. 29–30.
[10] Hildegard Adam, *Das Zollwesen im fränkischen Reich und seine Bedeutung für das
spätkarolingische Wirtschaftsleben* (Stuttgart, 1996), pp. 197–8.

'Legitimate' markets were controlled by the king, not only because a market toll was levied on the commercial transactions operated there, but also because the number of markets, especially during the reign of King Charles the Bald, had run out of control through the continuous founding of new markets.[11] This founding was possible without royal authorisation and frequently due to the initiative of a count, a church or a private landowner on his estate. The king took measures to concentrate commercial operations especially on his markets and to discourage those who avoided markets to escape tolls.[12] He therefore accorded guarantees of security, special protection, price control, etc. during market time. Some of the public markets were given to churches together with the market toll. Some were urban, as was the case with the market at Arras, given to the St Vaast abbey there,[13] but most were rural and established near the centre of an estate (so-called *villa*-markets). The royal manor of Bastogne, for example, in the Ardennes, was given to Our Lady's Church at Aachen in 887 by Charles (III) the Fat, together with its market.[14] Little is known about these rural markets, because official documents such as charters or capitularies are mostly silent about them. Buying and selling on them were indeed free from tolls when their object was the daily supply of victuals and utensils. Very famous, on the contrary, because of their international character were some fairs, above all the fair in October near the abbey of St Denis outside Paris.[15] Such a location, outside a town but still near to it and especially near to an abbey, was usual. During the fair of St Denis the king, since Dagobert's time (629–39), had conceded his right to levy tolls to the abbey. Besides this fair a weekly market functioned at St Denis[16] as was also the case at Champbeau where half of the toll from the annual market and the totality of the toll on weekly markets had been given by Charles the Bald to the churches of Langres and Dijon.[17]

---

[11] Nelson, *Charles the Bald*, p. 30

[12] Boretius (ed.), *Capitularia*, vol. I, no. 143 (AD 821), c.1: '*Volumus . . . ut nullus teloneum exigat nisi in mercatibus ubi communia commertia emuntur ac venundantur . . . Quod si aliquis constituta mercata fugiens, ne teloneum solvere cogatur . . .*'; Ganshof, 'Tonlieu', p. 491 and note 14.

[13] Georges Tessier (ed.), *Recueil des actes de Charles II le Chauve, roi de France*, 3 vols. (Paris, 1943–55), vol. II, no. 304 (AD 867).

[14] Adam, *Zollwesen*, p. 197.

[15] Lebecq, *Marchands frisons*, pp. 25–6.

[16] Tessier (ed.), *Actes*, no. 263 (AD 864).

[17] Nelson, *Charles the Bald*, p. 225.

Although much of the commercial activity within the Carolingian empire was located, much more than in later centuries, outside the towns, on rural and semi-rural markets and fairs, towns were even in the Carolingian period, in spite of the views of Pirenne, the favourite location of commerce. This is evident from the many toll privileges situating tolls in *civitates*, *castella*, *portus*, *vicus*, which, besides some points on the frontiers of the empire, were the most important toll stations. Most merchants, notwithstanding their mobility and their frequent absence from home, lived in towns. This was not only the case in Italy with its strong urban tradition. Since Antiquity there even the landed proprietors had lived within towns. It was also true in northwest Europe, where *civitates* such as Paris, Maastricht, Mainz and others have written and/or archaeological evidence of established merchants having their houses and storehouses there. But also in smaller and younger towns, often simply called *portus* or *vicus*, mentions of intensive parcelling indicated by the word *sessus*, *sedile*, denote the urban character of the place, which, together with the location of a toll, may be ascribed to its commercial function. In this context it is important to note that *civitates* of Roman origin were normally the seat of a bishop and that younger towns had often developed in the neighbourhood of a great abbey. The commercial role of these churches, with their potential of capital, power and privileges for their own commercial activity, which today is universally acknowledged, has in my opinion strongly contributed to the commercial character of the town next to them. Even the role of these towns as centres of artisanal activity, which was treated in Chapter 5, may be explained, at least partially, in this way. An analogous argument can be developed concerning the role of political power, especially of the king, in the origin of some new urban centres during the eighth and ninth centuries. Some royal palaces, not just Aachen, which is obviously a special case, but also those of minor importance, like at Valenciennes,[18] undoubtedly influenced the commercial function of the town next to them.

A very special case in this respect are the Carolingian *emporia*.[19] They have become famous under that specific name although not all of them bear it in the primary sources. Most famous within

[18] Verhulst, *Rise of Cities*, pp. 56–7.
[19] Hodges, *Dark Age Economics*, pp. 47–86; Hodges, *Towns and Trade*, pp. 69–92; Clarke and Ambrosiani, *Towns in the Viking Age*, pp. 11–45; Verhulst, 'Roman Cities, *Emporia* and New Towns', pp. 110–15.

the boundaries of the Carolingian empire were Quentovic on the mouth of the Canche south of Boulogne, not far from the French Channel coast; Dorestad, south-east of Utrecht between the rivers Lek and Oude Rijn, partially under the actual small town of Wijk-bij-Duurstede; and probably also *Walichrum*-Domburg now off the coast of Walcheren. Some minor *emporia*, probably dependent economically if not administratively on these three, were situated at *Witla*, at the mouth of the Maas near Rotterdam, and at Medemblik in north Holland, on the coast of the Zuiderzee, which was the normal waterway to Scandinavia. They were all, in fact, situated on the maritime border of the empire and functioned in international trade as gateways to England and northern Europe, as will be shown below. Important royal tolls of 10 per cent were established at Quentovic and Dorestad, similar to those on the passes (*ad clusas*) in the Alps on the way to Italy.

Quentovic and Dorestad share characteristics not only with their neighbouring smaller *emporia* but also with a number of very important trading places outside the Frankish empire, with which they traded, such as Hamwic on the English Channel coast near Southampton and Hedeby (Haithabu) near the actual town of Schleswig, south of the actual German–Danish frontier. The most striking characteristic of all these trading places is their ephemerality, because most of them disappeared physically, at the latest in the tenth century, and were not succeeded on the same location by a town of some importance. Their short-lived prosperity, mainly during the second half of the eighth and the first half of the ninth century, is linked to their protection by royal authority, of the Danish king at Hedeby and of the king of Wessex at Hamwic. The Frankish king had his representatives (*procuratores rei publicae*) at Dorestad and Quentovic. In the latter place the abbot of Fontenelle in 787, with the title of *procurator*, and in 858–68 a certain *illuster vir Grippo, prefectus emporii Quentovici* had authority as a sort of controller of foreign trade, customs and tolls. Their authority extended over other ports where an important royal toll was established at the entry of the empire, such as Rouen and Amiens (*per diversos portus ac civitates exigens tributa atque vectigalia, maxime in Quentawic*). The decline of Carolingian royal authority at the end of the ninth century sealed their ruin and destruction, which had begun earlier in the century by Viking attacks in the 830s on Dorestad, its transfer as fief to Danish nobles and, in the case of Quentovic, probably by floods and the elevation of the sea-level.[20] This was not the case for old *civitates* like Rouen, Amiens, Maastricht and Tournai nor for younger towns along the rivers (*portus*) in the interior, which unlike the Carolingian *emporia* would become the towns of the future.

Regarding transport the fundamental difference was of course between transport by ship or over land. The much debated question of which of the two systems prevailed in Carolingian times is perhaps not to the point. The choice indeed depended not only on variables such as distance, navigability, route system and other 'external' factors, but more particularly on the nature of the commodities transported. Bulk commodities such as grain, wine, salt, quernstones and olive oil had as a rule to be transported by ship, overseas and on rivers, although some cases of salt transported over land, even over some hundreds of miles, are known. Ships had capacities of up to 12 tons for river and coastal transport and from 10 to 30 tons for overseas shipping.[21] They were moved by sail or rowers, not only on sea, but normally hauled from the riverbank by men, either slaves, unfree or freely hired men, or by horses, in case of navigating upstream. This was usual, for example, on the Rhine, where about 839 Frisian merchants are said to have hauled their ship upstream with the help of slaves and where a woman is supposed to have done so with the help of a horse.[22] Carts over land could be loaded, for example with grain or salt, from 200 to 1,000 kg whereas lighter commodities, such as furs, textiles, wax and of course spices and other valuables, could be transported by shoulder, often by slaves, or on pack-animals. Slaves are always reported to have been driven over land routes, mostly over very long distances, from central and eastern Europe, over the Alps and over the Pyrenees to Italy and Spain.

Although there are examples of hired transport by free men, to which Adalhard, abbot of Corbie, in his *Statutes* foresaw the possibility of having recourse,[23] several abbeys had imposed transport services upon their tenants, either over land by carts or on rivers

[20] R. A. Hall, 'The Decline of the Wic?' in Slater (ed.), *Towns in Decline*, pp. 120–36, recently threw doubt upon this opinion.

[21] Heiko Steuer, 'Der Handel der Wikingerzeit zwischen Nord- und Westeuropa aufgrund archäologischer Zeugnisse', in Düwel and Jankuhn *et al.* (eds.), *Untersuchungen zu Handel und Verkehr*, IV, *Der Handel der Karolinger- und Wikingerzeit*, pp. 120–21.

[22] Lebecq, *Marchands frisons*, II, pp. 151–5.

[23] Verhulst and Semmler, 'Statuts d'Adalhard', p. 250 note 233.

by ships of which, in most cases, the abbey owned at least one and more often up to six and even twelve. Abbeys and cathedrals, among them St Germain-des-Prés, St Remi de Reims, St Martin de Tours, Prüm and the bishop of Orléans are well documented in this respect.[24] They had their ships or their tenants sailing the rivers Loire, Seine and Moselle, whereas the Rhine and the Danube, but not the Rhône, are often cited for their intense river traffic.

The Carolingian kings and emperors were very concerned about the infrastructure of traffic, not only with regard to their numerous military expeditions, but also to trade. In principle, the royal highways (*strata legittima*), which often were the continuation of Roman roads, had to be free of tolls. The same had to be observed on the more sandy pathways through the territory of rural estates (*nec per villas rodaticum vel pulveraticum*).[25] Bridges were the king's main concern: in principle they belonged to the state (*ad ius publicum*),[26] their building and repair being ordered by royal ban and controlled by a hierarchy of officials – and most of all by royal *missi*, to whom many capitularies about such questions were directed. There was however a tendency from about the middle of the ninth century onwards of granting bridges to churches, together with the toll which was often levied there on land passage or river traffic (a tax called *pontaticum*, which in principle was a retribution for the use of the bridge). In general the number of 'private' bridges, also those newly built by 'private' lords, increased, but this made control by the king's *missi* the more difficult and in-efficient. Several capitularies complain of the number of unjustified taxes thus levied and try to stabilise their number by referring to the *antiqua consuetudo*, meaning the bridges and taxes existing since time immemorial. The famous capitulary of Thionville (805)[27] opposes the old and just tolls (*antiqua et iusta telonea*) to the new and unjust (*nova seu iniusta*). The question is whether this evolution should be ascribed to the intensification of traffic and trade or simply to the decline of royal authority. It seems probable that both factors worked together.

There are not many written sources on other elements of infrastructure, such as river ports and harbours. There is however

[24] Devroey, 'Services de transport à Prüm' and 'Services de transport à Saint-Germain-des-Prés', both reprinted in Devroey, *Grand domaine carolingien*.

[25] Boretius (ed.), *Capitularia*, no. 57, c. 7.

[26] Tessier (ed.), *Actes de Charles le Chauve*, no. 18, AD 842.

[27] Boretius (ed.), *Capitularia*, no. 44, c.13.

archaeological evidence on them, especially for Dorestad.[28] Its harbour was situated east and alongside the left bank of the river Kromme Rijn. This branch of the Rhine had taken a crooked course and had constantly shifted eastward since the river Lek, in the first centuries of the Middle Ages, had tapped off much of its water. Excavations brought to light an extensive complex of wooden constructions that can be interpreted as wooden streets or causeways at right angles to the bank. Their construction must be connected with the development of the Rhine meander at this spot: they bridged the growing distance between the bank and the stream itself. Platforms, initially built against the bank, to which the ships could be brought, had to be lengthened constantly as the river shifted eastward. As they became longer the causeways were also extended further and further into the bays and finally assumed the character of jetties. The division of the harbour possibly influenced the structure of the town in the following way. The harbour parcels adjoining a road along the edge of the embankment, continued into the town on the other side of the road, each of them corresponding with a couple of jetties. On these parcels stood houses with their longitudinal axis towards the river. As there was room lengthwise for at least three houses, this part of the town consisted of three or more rows of houses, situated behind each other and parallel to the river bank.

Before passing on, in the next pages, to the different ranges and directions of commercial activities, what has been said at the beginning of this chapter on the nature of commerce in the Carolingian period, deserves repetition. From several sources, but especially those related to tolls on transport, on which much of our information will be based and which, for a large part, if not by nature or origin but by object and destination are ecclesiastical, commerce appears to have been practised in many cases by churches, not out of profit, but 'out of necessity'. Many churches had obtained freedom of tolls from the king, as had royal merchants at the king's service – except at the main toll stations of the empire (Quentovic, Dorestad and the Alpine passes (*ad clusas*)) where all had to pay the heavy tax of 10 per cent. Transport for the king's palaces and for the army was also free from tax. For toll receivers it must often have been difficult, even after

---

[28] W. Van Es, 'Dorestad Centred', in J. C. Besteman, J. M. Bos and H. A. Heidinga (eds.), *Medieval Archaeology in the Netherlands. Studies Presented to H. H. van Regteren Altena* (Assen and Maastricht, 1990), pp. 151–82.

inspection of the mostly rather vague formulation of the written toll freedom privilege, to differentiate, among the commodities transported for a church, between purely commercial goods and goods transported to be sold or bought, directly or indirectly, for own consumption. They often had to call on witnesses and declarations under oath. The difficulty may even have been greater if the transport was 'from one house to another' (*de una domo sua ad aliam*), for in such cases a privilege was not even necessary.[29]

[29] Ganshof, 'Tonlieu', p. 491 note 12.

7

DIRECTIONS OF TRADE

LOCAL AND INTER-REGIONAL TRADE

The difficulty of differentiating between purely commercial goods and goods to be sold or bought for own consumption was apparently not so great nor so frequent in the transports to local markets, which were representative of local or home trades. These local markets, generally situated in the countryside, were mostly visited by ordinary people who were free of taxes for victuals and utensils bought or sold in small quantities (*per deneratas*). The transport services of abbeys and churches, also greater in volume, were generally directed to more important markets, situated in urban centres. Except for a fortuitous anecdote in a saint's life, sources are normally silent about what happened in these small markets. Only occasionally are we thus informed of the commodities exchanged. These were wool, flax, finished textiles, iron objects, ploughshares and other agricultural instruments such as metallic sickles, or surpluses from the peasants' own production, mainly grain or seeds, horses and cattle. Normally these markets were held weekly but some grew in importance and developed into an annual fair. This was the case at St Hubert and Bastogne in the Ardennes.[1]

Inter-regional trade, between regions sometimes more than hundreds of kilometres distant from each other, had its stations, annual fairs excepted, in urban centres of different origin, size and

---

[1] Georges Despy, 'Villes et campagnes aux ixe et xe siècles: l'exemple du pays mosan', *Revue du Nord* 50 (1968), pp. 162–5.

importance. Some of them were old Roman *civitates*, like most Italian cities and many in southern Gaul (Marseilles, Arles, Narbonne, Lyon) and like Rouen, Paris, Amiens, Tournai, Cambrai, Maastricht, Mainz, respectively situated on the Seine, the Somme, the Maas and the Rhine. Others were smaller *castella* of Roman origin, like Huy and Dinant on the Meuse and many smaller towns on the Rhine and the Danube. That most of them were situated on waterways or along or near the coast is easily explained by the fact that their main merchandise was bulk commodities, mostly transported by ship.

Salt was certainly the most transported merchandise over large distances, partly because it was the main preserving product in those as in later ages and also because it was only found, exploited and produced in a few places. One of these places was in the salt pans around the mouth of the Loire and especially the Baie de Bourgneuf. They were exploited by private entrepreneurs, partially on account of the king.[2] From Nantes the salt was transported by ship along the Loire and its tributaries, past Angers, Tours, Orléans and Nevers. Salt is mentioned as an important element of the cargo of their ships in several charters of Charlemagne and Louis the Pious for abbeys situated on or near the Loire. Another element may have been grain. It seems doubtful that the totality of the transported salt was brought to the abbey and not sold partially en route. Sometimes, perhaps because of special climatic circumstances that affected the Loire river as well as some salt-producing places in north-eastern France, salt was brought there over land from the Atlantic coast.

Another salt-producing region, the exploitation of which was described in Chapter 5, was around Metz in north-eastern France. Several abbeys (Prüm, Aniane, Corvey, St Denis) possessed salt pans at Marsal and Vic-sur-Seille, the production of which was transported downstream on the river Moselle. The abbey of Prüm was the most involved in this production and transport. Obligatory transport services for this abbey brought not only salt, but also especially wine and grain, on rafts down the Moselle.

The best documented salt trade of the Carolingian period was that carried on by Bavarians on the river Danube between Passau and the eastern borders of the empire during the last quarter of the ninth century. An inquiry from 903–5, known as *Inquisitio Raffelstettensis* was made into the situation and tariffs at different toll stations in

---

[2] Ganshof, 'Tonlieu', p. 488 and above Chapter 5.

that area.[3] It reveals that inhabitants of Bavaria, who were not all professional merchants, were favoured against professional merchants from elsewhere (Jews and others) when they had to pay taxes when selling salt on public markets, especially at Linz. The salt was brought from the mines at Reichenhall by ship on the river Inn to Passau and from there downstream eastwards, beyond Linz, to legitimate markets (*mercatum constitutum*) in the Ostmark. There they could, after having paid the many transport tolls, carry on their trade without paying a market toll. Salt was also brought to the Ostmark on carts, over the *strata legittima*, where there was protection. Compensation for the many tolls between Passau and the eastern frontier of the empire was the freedom from tax for the Bavarians when they entered the empire again and sailed upstream. At this point their commerce was no longer intra- or inter-regional, but became international, with other commodities than just salt being exported and imported.

Places at the estuary of the river Po, such as Comacchio or to the north of it Venice, produced little more than salt. Initially, because a charter on that matter had been granted by the Lombard King Liutprand in 715, this salt was transported upstream along the Po to its confluence with the Oglio between Cremona and Mantua by agents of Comacchio privileged as *milites*. Soon though, in the second half of the ninth century, the Comacchesi were elbowed out of this traffic by traders from Cremona (852) and by Venetians who, in 862, owed payments to the office of the abbey of Bobbio in Mantua.[4]

Next to salt, grain was certainly the second bulk commodity most traded in inter-regional commerce. The most intriguing question about this trade is which regions, when not afflicted by famine, needed grain imports for their normal subsistence. The just-quoted salt-producing region around the Po estuary, gives a very appropriate answer. It produced little more than salt and had a great need for agrarian products. These were brought down the Po from the markets in Pavia, Piacenza, Cremona, Parma and Mantua, where big abbeys such as Bobbio, Sta Giulia di Brescia, Novalesa and others possessed subsidiaries to which they brought surpluses from their estates, especially corn and oil. These towns themselves were more populated than most towns in the more northern parts of the Carolingian empire

---

[3] François-L. Ganshof, 'Note sur l' "Inquisitio de theloneis Raffelstettensis" ', *Le Moyen Âge* 72 (1966), pp. 197–224; Adam, *Zollwesen*, pp. 124–7.

[4] Cinzio Violante, *La società milanese nell'età precommunale*, new edition (Rome, Bari, 1974), pp. 3–6.

and hence were grain consuming. Situated in the fertile valleys of the Po and its tributaries they did not, however, feed a grain trade over long distances and of inter-regional character.

The same cannot probably be said of the grain trade on the river Main upstream of its confluence with the Rhine at Mainz. It looks as if it was indeed fed by the city of Mainz and its supraregional importance. Merchants from Mainz, Einhard tells us, used to bring grain (*frumentum*) from the 'upper parts' of Germany, probably Upper Franconia and especially the region around Würzburg, by ship to Mainz.[5] This important city not only needed this supply from a region more than a hundred kilometres away because of the number of its inhabitants, but also because it was a grain market the reputation of which transcended just the Mainz region. In 850 the author of the *Annals of Fulda* was informed about the grain price on the market of Mainz, which was fairly high at that moment because of a famine in the Rhine region. These merchants however, also brought wine down the river Main. The question then arises whether part of this grain and wine was transported from Mainz further northward down the Rhine, especially when the presence in Mainz of a colony of Frisian merchants in the second half of the ninth century is taken into account. As Frisian merchants brought wine and grain from Alsace down the upper Rhine, and wine from the Worms region, it seems not impossible that on their way northward, passing by Mainz, they used its port for storage and loaded grain and wine coming to Mainz from Upper Franconia. Sailing further down the Rhine their final destination probably was Dorestad.[6] Excavations here brought to light oakwood identified as coming from Rheinhessen and white pinewood from Alsace, both from casks in which wine had been transported. Both for grain and wine Dorestad was the end of an inter-regional trade route, but at the same time the starting point for international export trade of grain and wine to northern Europe.[7] There is a discussion about whether the countryside around Dorestad had an agricultural production sufficient for a population that has been estimated not to be much higher than 1,500. While the supply of cattle seems to have been no problem, I doubt that Frisia, being a densely populated region with a very limited capacity for arable farming because of its

[5] Georg Waitz (ed.), *Translatio et Miracula SS. Marcellini et Petri*, MGH, SS.xv-1, p. 250, c. 6: '*mercatores quidam de civitate Mogontiaco, qui frumentum in superioribus Germaniae partibus emere ac per fluvium Moinum ad urbem devehere solebant.*'

[6] Lebecq, *Marchands frisons*, pp. 28, 226–7.

[7] Van Es, 'Dorestad Centred', pp. 163–72.

geographical condition, produced enough grain for a population that has been estimated at 30,000.[8] I therefore think that the inter-regional grain trade from the upper and middle Rhine region to Dorestad was not only for export overseas, but also for consumption in the region itself.

There were of course other regions where the same situation existed as in Frisia.[9] The north of medieval Flanders was in the ninth and still in the tenth and eleventh centuries a wooded area with large moorlands in between. Arable farming was not yet very developed and produced more oats than spelt, wheat or rye. The same was true of the Belgian Ardennes where, after the first clearances in the ninth century, oats were the principal produce. Nevertheless, towns like Ghent and Bruges, Maastricht and Huy, however small some of them were at their start in the ninth century, had to be supplied with grain from more fertile regions in southern Flanders or southern Brabant. The rich abbey of St Bavo's at Ghent can rightly be supposed to have brought grain from its estates in southern Flanders and northern France, along the rivers Leie and Scheldt to Ghent, not only for the abbey's consumption, but probably also to be sold to the urban population.

Abbot Adalhard of Corbie in his famous *Statutes* of 822 making sound calculations of the grain supply needed from the abbey's estates for the monastery's huge population, still ordered that grain from estates farther than 30 km away, should not be brought to the abbey, but sold on the spot. This may also have fed an inter-regional grain trade to the neighbouring towns of Amiens, Cambrai and Arras. To differentiate it from local trade is rather difficult in these cases.

Differentiation between inter-regional trade and international commerce is also particularly difficult for that other bulk commodity, wine. What has been said about the grain trade from Alsace and the middle Rhine region to Dorestad, is true for wine from those regions, which was often associated with it, as shown above. The same association occurred in the transport of (mainly) wine and also grain by ship and rafts on the Moselle downstream of Trier on behalf of the abbey of Prüm at the end of the ninth century. Another very important wine-producing region where inter-regional trade fed international commerce, was along the upper and middle Seine. The abbey of St Germain-des-Prés possessed so many vineyards

[8] Lebecq, *Marchands frisons*, pp. 125–9.   [9] See Chapter 1.

here that its production, estimated at 15,000 mud, greatly exceeded
the needs of its own consumption, which were estimated at 2,000
mud.[10] This enormous surplus was brought into commerce and for
a large part transported along the Seine to Paris by means of transport services for the abbey. The latter may have sold it on the fair
of St Denis, in October after the vintage, which was the greatest
wine market of western Europe. Since the middle of the eighth century Frisians and (Anglo-) Saxons visited it to buy and export wine.
The fair of St Denis, where also wine from the abbey of St Denis itself
must have been sold, thus had somewhat the same role as Dorestad:
the end of an inter-regional trade route and the starting point of
international commerce.[11]

The possession of vineyards in wine-producing regions by abbeys
not themselves situated in such regions and at great distances from
the seat of the abbey has been used by the late professor Hans Van
Werveke, one of Pirenne's students and his successor at Ghent university, as a decisive proof of the absence of commerce in Carolingian
times.[12] It is impossible here to refute his whole argument, but some
points in it must be criticised in the context of our exposition. Van
Werveke cannot of course deny the wine trade of the Frisians, but
he limits its effects to Holland, arguing that Dutch abbeys had no
distant vineyards because, thanks to the Frisian wine trade, they did
not need them. The abbeys in present-day Belgium to which he
limits his article, on the contrary, would not have been touched by
this Frisian trade! Considering the list of geographically distant vineyards of 'Belgian' abbeys in the Carolingian period, one gets the
impression that they were not very important, even if exceptionally
situated in the well-known wine-producing regions along the Rhine
and the Seine. Most were situated around Laon and Soissons, north
of Paris.

The export of quern-stones from the volcanic basalt quarries of
Niedermendig near Mayen and shipped from nearby Andernach to
Dorestad was an inter-regional transport of bulk that debouched into

[10] Elmshäuser and Hedwig, *Studien zum Polyptychon von Saint-Germain-des-Prés*,
pp. 365–99.
[11] Lebecq, *Marchands frisons*, pp. 25–6.
[12] Hans Van Werveke, 'Comment les établissements religieux belges se procuraient-
ils du vin au haut moyen âge?', *Revue belge de philologie et d'histoire* 2 (1923),
pp. 643–62, reprinted in Van Werveke, *Miscellanea Mediaevalia*, pp. 12–29.

an international trade.[13] Many hundreds of fragments have been excavated at Dorestad, where these stones were of course not all used, but finished off to be exported on a large scale to England and northern Europe. They have been excavated in great numbers at Hamwic, London, York, Ribe and Hedeby, and can be identified with the 'black stones' (*petrae nigrae*) Charlemagne wrote about in his famous letter of 796 to King Offa of Mercia, to ask what size he wanted.[14]

Ceramics mainly originated from the middle Rhine south of Cologne, near Brühl, particularly the famous Badorf ware from *c.* 725 onwards to the end of the ninth century. During a shorter period (*c.* 775–*c.* 825), the so-called Tating jars spread over a large part of south and south-east England, especially at Hamwic, and in northern Europe, especially at Hedeby and Birka. Their production, clearly orientated to export, was also providing a bulk commodity in inter-regional trade.[15] The well-known *Miracles of St Goar* by Wandelbert, *c.* 839,[16] tells the adventure of a group of potters, transporting pots on the Rhine, with the intention of selling them in retail trade. It is likely that they sailed upstream near St Goar, probably coming from Brühl or Andernach. The pots were empty; being transported by potters, it is unlikely that they would have contained wine. These circumstances clearly point at a regional trade in ceramics.

INTERNATIONAL TRADE

Several examples of inter-regional trade quoted above have shown a link to international trade, some to the extent that in fact they may be considered as part of an international current. This was particularly the case on the Rhine route, which was the most important connection between north and south Europe in Carolingian times. In this respect it was the successor of the Rhône valley in the Merovingian period. The main cause for this shift is the decline of the ports of Provence in their role of intermediary for the trade between Italy and northern Europe.

This decline cannot be explained in the first place by the Arab conquest of the western Mediterranean, as Pirenne thought. We now

[13] Steuer, 'Handel aufgrund archäologischer Zeugnisse', pp. 142–6.
[14] This traditional interpretation has recently been challenged: Hodges, *Towns and Trade*, pp. 64–6.
[15] Steuer, 'Handel aufgrund archäologischer Zeugnisse', pp. 134–42.
[16] Lebecq, *Marchands frisons*, II, pp. 150–1.

know, through the research of D. Claude on commerce in the western Mediterranean since late Antiquity[17] and by the work of Simon
Loseby on Marseilles,[18] that the decline of the Provençal ports started
much earlier and had already reached a very low point in the seventh
century. But the decline was not uniform.[19] Some of Marseilles'
connections in the Mediterranean persisted beyond the Arab conquest, well into the eighth century. Several diplomatic missions from
Rome came by sea to Marseilles, especially during the years of
tension between the Carolingians and the king of the Lombards in
the third quarter of the eighth century, when the latter had closed
the passes over the Alps. Economically, however, this did not mean
much, not even the presence of an Anglo-Saxon merchant named
Botto in Marseilles around 750. In the second quarter and the middle
of the ninth century Arab raids seriously endangered overseas traffic
to the Provençal ports, especially to Marseilles and Arles and around
the isles of Corsica, Sardinia and Majorca. A dramatic illustration
of this situation was the sinking by the Arabs in 820, reported by
the royal Frankish annals, of eight merchant ships on their way from
Sardinia to Italy. This incident is characteristic of the contradictory
situation in the western Mediterranean at that time: although the
danger was great, commerce went on, albeit on a reduced scale. It
helps perhaps to understand the contradictions between the archaeological gap in the habitat of Marseilles, and in its minting during
the eighth and ninth centuries on the one hand, and some written evidence on the other, pointing to some economic activity. This
documentary evidence partly comes from the important abbey of
St Victor at Marseilles. Not only is there the famous polyptych of
St Victor, from the beginning of the ninth century, revealing the dynamic demographical situation of a young population but also some
toll privileges. If the gift of the toll of Lion on the étang de Berre to
the abbey of St Victor in 822 may still be interpreted as the sign of the
growing importance of a smaller local port and market as a competitor
to the neighbouring port of Marseilles, the gift to St Victor in 841 of

---

[17] Dietrich Claude, *Der Handel im westlichen Mittelmeer während des Frühmittelalters*
(Göttingen, 1985) (*Untersuchungen zu Handel und Verkehr der vor- und frühgeschicht-
lichen Zeit in Mittel- und Nordeuropa*, vol. 2, Abhandlungen Akademie Göttingen,
Phil.-Hist. Klasse, 3rd series, no. 144).

[18] Simon T. Loseby, 'Marseille and the Pirenne Thesis II: "Ville Morte"', in Hansen
and Wickham (eds.), *The Long Eighth Century*, pp. 167–93.

[19] Francois-L. Ganshof, 'Note sur les ports de Provence', *Revue Historique* 183 (1938),
pp. 28–37.

the toll on ships from Italy, mooring at the Vieux-port of Marseilles at the foot of St Victor's abbey and the freedom of toll given to the abbey of St Denis by Charles the Bald in 845 for goods bought or sold at Marseilles, indicate that the city had not totally lost its function in international commerce. Its function as a central place, however, especially in the ecclesiastical sphere, shifted into the interior, away from the sea, to the more inland situated port of Arles in the second half of the ninth century. In 878 Pope John VIII, with three ships from Naples and after an intermediate stop at Genoa, called at the port of Arles.[20]

The end of the ninth and the beginning of the tenth century marked for nearly a century, with the Arab conquest of Sicily, the Arab domination of the western Mediterranean. This did not ex-clude traffic and commerce over land, particularly with Spain and even with the Arabs themselves. Arles had an important role in it as intermediary as early as the beginning of the ninth century. The poet Theodulf, himself of Spanish origin, saw at Arles in 812 luxury goods, like leather from Cordoba, silk, jewels and also Arab coins, brought to that place by Arab merchants.[21] Quicksilver, used for jew-ellery making in western Europe, must also have been imported from Spanish mines. Slaves, captured from central and eastern Europe by Charlemagne's campaigns against the Saxons, Danes, Slavonic tribes and Avars, and brought via Verdun, Lyon and Narbonne, to Arles, were exported, mainly by Jews, some of Spanish origin, to Saragossa and Cordoba, via Ampurias and Gerona and the Pyrenees pass of Le Perthuis.[22]

The shift from the sea route between Italy and the Provençal ports to the Alpine passes was accelerated by the Frankish conquest in 774 of the Lombard kingdom in Italy. In the following year the abbey of St Denis was privileged with freedom from the toll levied under the name *exclusaticum* at the Alpine passes most used by the abbey, prob-ably the Mont Cenis or the Great St Bernard pass. These were the passes for the traffic from northern France and the Rhineland into Italy.[23] From Bavaria and the most eastern provinces of the Frankish

---

[20] Ganshof, 'Ports de Provence', pp. 32–3.
[21] R. Doehaerd, *Le Haut Moyen Âge Occidental. Economie et sociétés* (Paris, 1971), p. 278. Transl.: *Early Middle Ages in the West. Economy and Society* (New York 1978).
[22] Charles Verlinden, *L'esclavage dans l'Europe médievale*, I, *Peninsule ibérique-France* (Bruges, 1955: Rijksuniversiteit Gent. Werken Fac. Letteren en Wijsbegeerte 119), pp. 709–17.
[23] Ganshof, 'Tonlieu', pp. 492–3 and note 16.

empire into Italy several more eastward passes, known as the 'Bündner passes', in the modern Swiss canton of Graubünden (among them the Septimer and the Julier), were used. The tolls levied at these passes (*ad clusas*), probably since late Antiquity and maintained by the Lombard king, were considered frontier tolls, even after the incorporation of the Lombard kingdom in the Frankish empire.[24] Like those at Quentovic and Dorestad and probably also at the Perthuis pass to Spain, they amounted to the considerable tax of 10 per cent *ad valorem* and were the most important of the empire. We know more however about the crossing of the Alps by Charlemagne himself, the pope and their envoys, than about commercial traffic on these routes. It may be considered for the larger part as international, although the Lombard kingdom was since 774 part of the Frankish empire. The internal economy of the Lombard kingdom was like that of Provence in the eighth and ninth centuries, not very dynamic, notwithstanding the continuity of urban life in the cities of northern Italy. The incentives for international commercial traffic from Italy northward over the Alps and vice versa came from the theoretically Byzantine, but practically independent territories and cities: chiefly Venice, but also Naples, Amalfi, Otranto and, in another context, Rome, which with its 25,000 inhabitants was still the largest city of Italy.[25] By the end of the eighth century the depressing effects of Byzantine control over the central Mediterranean had ceased and commercial relations with the eastern Mediterranean intensified. The treaty of 812 between Charlemagne and the Emperor Michael of Byzantium gave Venice great possibilities in the eastern basin of the Mediterranean.[26] At the beginning of the ninth century the city emerged as the successor of Marseilles as port of trade for east-Mediterranean goods. It now enjoyed protection from the Carolingian kings of Italy, as it had from their Lombard predecessors, and in 840 from the emperor Lotharius. The *pactum Lotharii* exempted Venice from toll and berthing taxes (*ripaticum*) and made it possible for its merchants to expand to the central and northern parts of the Frankish empire, while traders from the latter were given concessions in the shipping trade

---

[24] P. Duparc, 'Les cluses et la frontière des Alpes', *Bibliothèque de l'École des Chartes* 109 (1951), pp. 5–31; Gaston G. Dept, 'Le mot 'clusas' dans les diplômes carolingiens', in *Mélanges d'histoire offerts à Henri Pirenne*, 1 (Brussels, 1926), pp. 89–98; Johanek, 'Fränkische Handel', p. 16 and note 39.

[25] Wickham, *Land and Power*, pp. 108–16.

[26] Violante, *Societá milanese*, pp. 6–10.

by the Venetians and even participated in the Venetian commercial enterprises with money. Venetian merchants around 780 brought to Pavia, the king's capital in Italy, silk and Byzantine textiles (*pallia*). A century later, Notker Balbulus, the famous monk and story-teller from St Gall, mentions as imports from the Near East in Pavia silk, purpur from Tyrus, ermine and from Persia balm, unguent, perfumes, medicine and pigment. As early as 750, according to the *Liber Pontificalis*, Venetians travelled to Rome in order to buy slaves for export, probably to North Africa. From Alexandria Venetian merchants in 827 brought the relics of St Marc to their city. It seems likely that goods from eastern Europe, imported through Bohemia and the Avar territory into the Ostmark (actual Austria) and Bavaria over the Danube, reached Venice over the Bündner passes and were exported to the eastern Mediterranean.[27] From a polyptych describing royal estates around 842–3 in the region of Chur (actual north-east Switzerland), we know that a toll at Walenstadt, on the Walensee, was levied on slaves and horses, probably imported from eastern Europe through Bavaria, which were brought over the Alpine passes into Italy and most likely, because of the geographic orientation, to Venice. A confirmation of the position of Walenstadt on the route to Italy can be found in a letter by Alcuin from 791–6 to the bishop of Chur, asking for his intervention against the receivers of the toll in favour of his personal merchant (*negotiator*) bringing home goods from Italy (*Italiae mercimonia*).[28]

The international character of the commerce of the Byzantine cities in southern Italy was perhaps geographically less extensive than that of Venice, although the slaves raided in 836 in the Beneventan territory by merchants from Naples were to be exported to Egypt. Our information on goods imported through Venice or other Italian ports from the eastern Mediterranean into western Europe in the Carolingian period is nearly non-existent. Apart from one mention of a transport of olive oil on the Rhine, there is one controversial text concerning the presence at the market of Cambrai of spices and other special oriental wares, which the person for whom the text was written had to buy 'if there was money enough'. Although preserved in a manuscript dated between 822 (because the text is preceded by the famous *Statutes* of abbot Adalhard of Corbie of that year) and

---

[27] Dopsch, *Wirtschaftsentwicklung*, II, pp. 202–10; Doehaerd, *Haut Moyen Âge*, pp. 277–81.

[28] Dopsch, *Wirtschaftsentwicklung*, II, pp. 201–2.

986, Pirenne and several authors after him considered the text as typical Merovingian and used it for contrasting that period to the Carolingian period, when according to them such a text had been impossible. I am not convinced by such a circular argument and, without having a definite opinion for the moment, I do not think it impossible that the text may be of the date of the manuscript and related, in one way or another, to the *Statutes* of Adalhard of Corbie.[29]

The unstable political and military situation in and around the Mediterranean during the eighth and ninth centuries, the lack of internal dynamics of the Lombard part of Italy (notwithstanding the rise of Venice and its relations and those of other Byzantine cities in Italy with the eastern Mediterranean), the decline around the Mediterranean of the production of fine ceramics suitable for export to western Europe and thus for archaeological investigation there – these are all factors that can explain the scarcity of evidence for the import of Mediterranean products into western Europe under the Carolingians. The cause is not a single one like the Arab invasions and raids invoked by Pirenne, but a complex of factors, among which the Arabs are one, the effect of which was to shift the centre of gravity to north-west and northern Europe, as Pirenne had rightly seen. However, the dynamic economy of these northern regions produced archaeological evidence which Pirenne could not have known and to which we will turn now.

Our knowledge of trade relations between the Frankish empire and northern Europe, mainly with England and Scandinavia, is for the larger part based on archaeological evidence, confirmed from time to time by written texts.[30] The products exported from the Carolingian empire to the north – ceramics, glass, quern-stones, metallic objects – are mainly archaeological whereas those imported from the north – furs, hides and fells, wax and amber, even slaves – have never or seldom left material traces. From this one gets the impression that there was more imported into England and Scandinavia than exported from these countries to the Carolingian empire, an impression that might be correct. The numerous Carolingian coins found in the north may well be related to tributes paid to the Vikings and do not necessarily reflect an unequal balance of payments.

---

[29] Verhulst, *Rise of Cities*, p. 58.
[30] Steuer, 'Handel aufgrund archäologischer Zeugnisse'.

Since the middle of the eighth century most merchants operating on the North Sea were Frisians and the history of commerce on and around the North Sea is mainly theirs.[31] They were also operating along the Rhine between Dorestad and the Alps. In different cities along that river, in Worms, Mainz, Duisburg and Birten near Xanten, they had established colonies during the second half of the ninth century. Apart from the isolated presence of a Frisian merchant in London before the end of the seventh century, their collective and regular appearance at the fair of St Denis since at least 753, in the track of English merchants, marks the beginning of their domination of northern commerce. They came there to buy wine from the Seine region and it is probable that, as well as transporting it to their Frisian homeland, they exported it outside Carolingian borders as they did wine from Alsace, the remains of the wooden casks of which were excavated at Hedeby. We do not know, however, if the wine from the Paris region was transported in wooden casks or in jars and amphores of the Badorf type, the oldest sherds of which in England were found in London and date from *c.* 775. The Badorf ceramics were produced near Brühl, south of Cologne, and their use at the St Denis fair is not certain at all. It is archaeologically impossible to determine if the jars and amphores of the Badorf type were exported for themselves as luxury goods or were filled with wine. However, their shards were found in great numbers at the *emporium* of Hamwic on the English Channel coast near Southampton, just opposite the mouth of the Seine downstream of Rouen. The same is true, but for a shorter period ending around 825, for the famous jars of so-called Tating ware, which were produced in the region of Niedermendig, between the Rhine and the Moselle not far from Koblenz and Andernach. Both types of ceramic were also exported to Scandinavia, where at both Ribe and Hedeby they represent 5 to 7 per cent of the ceramic finds.[32] Further north, they have also been found at Kaupang, near Oslo, and particularly at Birka, the important port of trade on the isle of Björkö in lake Mälar in central Sweden. To this place, however distant, they were brought no doubt by Frisian merchants, because the relations between Birka and Dorestad were particularly intense at the end of the eighth and the beginning of the ninth century. The main written source for this assertion is the *Vita Anskarii* from 865–76, the

[31] Lebecq, *Marchands frisons*.
[32] Ulf Näsman, 'Exchange and Politics: the Eighth–Early Ninth Century in Denmark', in Hansen and Wickham (eds.), *Long Eighth Century*, pp. 46–7.

Life of Anschar, archbishop of Bremen-Hamburg, who evangelised
the Birka region. It tells the story of a rich lady with the Frisian
name Frideburg, living at Birka, who, in around 845–50, asked her
daughter Catla in her will to give away her fortune to the (allegedly)
many churches of Dorestad and to the poor there.[33] At Hedeby too,
according to the same source, there were many Christians baptised
in Dorestad or Hamburg and who belonged to the upper class of
the place. In England, mostly in London and Hamwic, and in Ribe,
Hedeby, Kaupang and Uppland Sweden (Uppsala), Rhenish glass
and glass from the Ardennes, notably funnelled cups and pearls, were
found, the latter being also manufactured in Ribe itself, perhaps by
a wandering artisan.

Whereas these were luxury goods, the same is certainly not true
for the black quern-stones, manufactured from the lava pits at
Niedermendig, near Mayen, and shipped on the Rhine northward
from the embarkment port of Andernach.[34] They were of one type
(40–50 cm in diameter), from England to Jutland, where their fragments have been found in all the *emporia*. In England, where even
King Offa (as appears from a letter of Charlemagne to him) was interested in what were called the 'black stones' (*petrae nigrae*),[35] they were
distributed over the countryside, mostly in south-east England. There
is no doubt that they were shipped and traded by Frisians. Many hundreds of fragments were found in Dorestad, more than enough for just
domestic use. Their manufacture stopped shortly after the beginning
of the ninth century. Although the famous Frankish swords, with decorated grip and blade with inscriptions, manufactured in the Meuse
and Rhine region (Cologne), have been found all over Europe, they
were particularly cherished in Scandinavia.[36] It is, however, difficult
to prove that they came there as a product of commerce, for except at Dorestad, they were not found in the *emporia* and may have
reached the Scandinavian and also the south-east English countryside
as loot brought home by Vikings. Moreover one should not forget
that an interdiction on weapon export from the Frankish empire was
repeated often in the capitularies of Charlemagne and his successors.

Textiles have left little or no archaeological traces at all. Apart
from some fragments found in excavations in Birka, Kaupang and

[33] Lebecq, *Marchands frisons*, I, pp. 31–2; II, pp. 131–3.
[34] Steuer, 'Handel aufgrund archäologischer Zeugnisse', pp. 142–6.
[35] Hodges, *Towns and Trade*, pp. 64–6 mentions another interpretation of the '*petrae nigrae*'.
[36] Steuer, 'Handel aufgrund archäologischer Zeugnisse', pp. 151–6.

Hedeby, the idea that textiles must have been the object of trade relations between the Frankish empire, England and Scandinavia is based on some fortuitous allusions in written sources. Best known are the mentions of *pallia Fresonica* and *saga Fresonica* in the *Gesta Karoli* of Notker Balbulus, the monk and story-teller of St Gall around 886–7.[37] They consisted of various colours and are considered by most specialists as luxury cloth, the quality of which was fine enough to be offered by Charlemagne to Harun ar-Rashid, the caliph of Baghdad. The poem dedicated in the 820s by Ermold the Black to Pipin, king of Aquitaine, expressly states that merchants brought from Frisia into Alsace coats of various colours. After many polemical discussions started by Pirenne, for whom Frisian cloth had been manufactured in Flanders and only been transported by Frisian merchants, Stéphane Lebecq, the French specialist of Frisian history, concluded, on archaeological grounds, that these textiles had been manufactured in Frisia itself. Some authors before him had argued that they had been exported from England to the continent by Frisians. Their arguments, apart from the Frisian question, prove that English textiles were indeed exported to the continent. In his famous letter to Offa, king of Mercia, from shortly after 796, Charlemagne, in exchange for his intervention concerning the 'black stones' asked for by Offa, asks the latter that the coats exported from England into Francia should again have their usual length. Perhaps less famous but no less significant in this context, is a gift to the abbey of St Bertin in 800 of a sum of money to buy cloth for shirts from overseas called *bernicrist* in vernacular (*drappos ad kamisias ultromarinas que vulgo bernicrist vocitantur*).[38]

Frankish trade with central and eastern Europe must be situated in a different political and military context than that with England or even Scandinavia, mainly because the frontier on this side of the empire, formed through central and south-east Germany by the rivers Elbe, Saale and Donau, was not only a political one but also a military frontline, the control of which was very strict. There is evidence in different capitularies, especially in that of Thionville (805), of trade control and probably also tolls in different places on these rivers, from Bardowiek and Magdeburg on the Elbe, Erfurt, Hallstadt and Forcheim on the Saale, to Regensburg and Lorch on the Donau.[39]

---

[37] Lebecq, *Marchands frisons*, pp. 131–4.
[38] Maurits Gysseling and Anton Koch (eds.), *Diplomata belgica ante annum millesimum centesimum scripta* (Tongeren, 1950), p. 41.
[39] Johanek, 'Fränkische Handel', pp. 15–18, 37.

More specifically the sale and smuggling of coats of mail called *brunia*, was severely repressed. The situation was less tense at the south-eastern border of the empire, east of Bavaria, at the eastern frontier of the so-called Ostmark, a Frankish military buffer territory against the Avars. The situation in this corner of the empire is well known from the inquiry from 903–5 concerning the toll of Raffelstetten, which we studied above from the point of view of inter-regional trade. It provides evidence of import by Czechs and Russians of slaves, horses and wax, that came via a route Kiev–Cracow–Prague. Most of these imports were directed via Arlberg to Walenstadt on the Walensee in north-east Switzerland and from there over one of the 'Bündner' passes to Venice, as I made clear in my overview on the international trade position of Venice.

CONCLUSION

To conclude it can be stated that inter-regional trade was more important than the international commerce of the Carolingian empire. The latter was concentrated in places along the frontier of the Frankish empire, where important royal tolls were established, and in the theoretically Byzantine cities and territories of Italy, most of all in Venice. There is not much information about the goods imported and exported in southern Europe: the main export to the former Byzantine possessions in Italy and from there to Muslim North Africa consisted of slaves; the export of slaves from north-west Europe via some cities in southern France to Muslim Spain was equally important; the import of oriental spices, perfumes and silk via Venice and some other formerly Byzantine ports in Italy and from Muslim Spain to the Provence may not be overestimated.

In Europe north of the Alps and the Loire, the international circuit was much interwoven with inter-regional trade, especially on the Rhine, from the Alps to Dorestad, the main gateway to Scandinavia. Exports to Scandinavia, consisting of glass ware, ceramics, quernstones and textiles were more important than imports from Scandinavia, of which we know nearly nothing. Trade with England, through Quentovic and *Walichrum*–Domburg and also through Dorestad, was more an extension of inter-regional trade, with exports of mainly wine and ceramics and quern-stones to England and with imports of textiles from England to the continent.

Compared with international commerce, inter-regional trade movements are not only much better documented, especially thanks to written sources rather than archaeological evidence (except ceramics and quern-stones), but this superiority corresponds to a reality that is most visible in northern France, the Low Countries and the Rhineland – the heartlands of the Carolingian empire. Inter-regional commerce, which was much more important than earlier scholars, especially Pirenne, would have us believe, had its roots in the great estates of those regions. They produced a surplus of grain, wine and salt that were the main basic commodities transported over the rivers Rhine, Loire, Seine, Meuse, Moselle and Main. The best explanation of this commercial flowering in north-west Europe during the Carolingian period, which in the end must have stimulated international exports to England and Scandinavia, is the dynamism of the Carolingian manorial economy and its merchant class. This consisted mainly of Frisian merchants who were at the service of this economy and its mainly ecclesiastical masters but at the same time had been left enough freedom for their own profitable operations.

PART IV

THE DYNAMICS OF THE CAROLINGIAN ECONOMY

8

MONEY AND PRICE MOVEMENTS

———— • ————

Before addressing the general and difficult problem of the use of money under the Carolingians the strict monetary history of their reign will be summarised in order to put the facts before their interpretation.[1]

In 754–5, soon after his accession to the throne as king, Pipin III restored the standard weight of the silver *denier*, which had progressively replaced the gold *tremissis* during the last decades of the seventh century, from 1.1 g to 1.3 g. Charlemagne during the first decades of his reign, from 768 to 793–4, did not innovate and maintained this weight, only reducing the number of mints to about forty. Apart from changes of the obverse and reverse of coins in 806, adapting them to Charles' imperial status, the only monetary reform of his reign until his death in 814 was in the winter of 793–4, when he increased the weight of the denier from 1.3 g to 1.7 g. The introduction of a heavy denier was not easily accepted by the public because it favoured the creditors at the expense of the debtors whose fixed obligations, for example as rentpayers, were apparently not changed. The explanation

---

[1] Philip Grierson, 'Money and Coinage under Charlemagne', in Wolfgang Braunfels, Helmut Beumann, Hermann Schnitzler and Bernhard Bischoff (eds.), *Karl der Grosse. Lebenswerk und Nachleben*, 4 vols. (Düsseldorf, 1965), vol. I, pp. 501–36, reprinted in Philip Grierson, *Dark Age Numismatics* (London, 1979), no. XVIII; Philip Grierson and Mark Blackburn, *Medieval European Coinage: with a Catalogue of the Coins in the Fitzwilliam Museum Cambridge*, vol. I: *The Early Middle Ages (fifth–tenth centuries)* (Cambridge, New York, 1986), pp. 190–266.

of what looks like a compensation for a lower silver price has been sought by Grierson, Doehaerd,[2] Bolin, Lombard[3] and others in the international relations of the Carolingian empire, particularly in the evolution of the relation of gold to silver in the east–west export trade. The high value of gold in the east as the consequence of the exclusive goldminting would have brought silver back to western Europe. But was this export trade so important, one may ask, that it influenced the flux of gold and silver between east and west? Cannot the (new) exploitation of the silver mines at Melle near Poitiers have had this effect on the silver price? Or should one take into account the rise of grain prices consequent on a famine in 792–3, less than a year before the monetary reform of the winter of 793–4, assuming that the purchasing power of the new coin had increased with its weight? The most recent and generally accepted explanation, put forward by Grierson–Blackburn, is that the monetary reform of 793–4 was an element in a general reform of weights and measures carried through at the same time and increasing the capacity of the *modius* by 50 per cent. Compared to the increase of the denier by 30 per cent, in weight and probably also in silver and purchasing power, the link seems evident. A half-denier or obol was simultaneously struck for the first time, apparently satisfying the economic need for a less valuable coin. In May 794 the Council of Frankfurt following the famine of the preceding year, fixed the maximum prices of grain and bread according to the new *modius* and enjoined the universal acceptance of the *novi denarii*. Not only is this resolution of the highest ecclesiastical authority proof of the moral basis of the Carolingian policy in economic matters, but also of the difficulties encountered by Charlemagne in pushing through his monetary reform. The penalties laid down by the Council of Frankfurt had indeed to be repeated in 809 as part of a whole monetary legislation formed by the many instructions in the capitularies on these matters. Counterfeiting was also one of the evils to be combatted: the restriction of minting to the palace, laid down in the famous capitulary of Thionville in 805, was repeated at Nijmegen in 808. But this position, which had been intended to put an end to counterfeiting, was soon weakened by acceding to the requests of local mints to reopen because of shortage of coin. Recoinage was

---

[2] Renée Doehaerd, 'Les réformes monétaires carolingiennes', *Annales. Economies–Sociétés–Civilisations* 7(1952), pp. 13–20, reprinted in Renée Doehaerd, *Oeconomica Mediaevalia* (Brussels, 1984), pp. 149–57.

[3] Bolin, 'Mohammad, Charlemagne'; Lombard, 'Les bases monétaires'.

another means of combatting counterfeiting, if at least demonetisation of old coins succeeded. This was the case under Louis the Pious, whose monetary policy, in contrast with the traditional image of a weak and ineffectual ruler, was characterised by uniformity and strength of control.[4] Three recoinages, first in 814 after the death of his father, then in 818, when the weight of the denier was increased to 1.8 g, but brought back to 1.7 g at the next recoinage in 822–3, succeeded and the demonetised issues were swiftly removed from circulation. This points to a rapid circulation throughout the whole empire, a sign of the favourable economic situation. The opening of the first (and for a long time the only) mint east of the Rhine at Regensburg in 817, however negligible its output may have been, is symbolic in this respect. Obols, well suited for small transactions, were also particularly numerous during the reign of Louis the Pious.

After the political fragmentation of 843 there was a loosening of control, less uniformity in design and fabric and a more localised circulation.[5] There was also a fall in the alloy of the denier, which during the first years of Charles the Bald contained only 50 per cent silver. The reform however, introduced by him in 864 by what has been called the 'edict' of Pîtres, produced an important reinforcement of the money: the uniform coinage of a new denier (type *Gratia Dei Rex GDR*) containing 96 per cent of silver. It was however, soon followed by a debasement and shortage of silver for more than a hundred years.[6] Several mints did not strike coins for nearly a century (Maastricht from 882–7 to 973–83; Visé from 877–9 until 983–6; Namur and Dinant from 900–911 to 983).

Although the payments of tribute to the Norsemen, which started in 845 (7,000 pounds), took place before the edict of Pîtres, namely in 853, 861 (5,000 pounds) and 862 (6,000 pounds), but continued after it (in 866, 4,000 pounds),[7] there has been some controversy over how far the Scandinavian invasions have been responsible for

[4] Simon Coupland, 'Money and Coinage under Louis the Pious', *Francia* 17(1990), pp. 23–54.

[5] Simon Coupland, 'The Early Coinage of Charles the Bald', *Numismatic Chronicle* 151(1991), pp. 121–58.

[6] Philip Grierson, 'The *Gratia Dei Rex* Coinage of Charles the Bald', in M. T. Gibson and J. L. Nelson (eds.), *Charles the Bald. Court and Kingdom*, second revised edition (London, 1990), pp. 52–64; D. M. Metcalf, 'A Sketch of the Currency in the Time of Charles the Bald', in Gibson and Nelson (eds.), *Charles the Bald*, pp. 65–97.

[7] Simon Coupland, 'The Frankish Tribute Payments to the Vikings and their Consequences', *Francia* 26 (1999), pp. 57–75.

the decline in coinage, particularly after the edict. Although it is not clear if these sums were paid in coin – Grierson even thinks that new mints were opened to provide coins to pay these taxes – it is doubtful whether the Danes, carrying off so much silver, returned it later to circulation in the west. It is possible on the contrary that the Danish invasions created a shortage of coins and silver, which was responsible for the opening of more mints of local significance, for a slower and more local circulation, reflected in the many hoards of those years, and for the reduction of the alloy.

So far Italy has been left out of the picture because it had a largely different monetary history.[8] This was due to the strong continuity with its Byzantine past and to the fact that the Frankish denier was a foreign currency imposed by the edict of Mantua in 781, some years after the Frankish conquest of northern and central Italy. Until then small bronze and silver coins, beside gold for the big trans-actions, had been struck in the Byzantine tradition. The denier of Charlemagne was much heavier than these small silver coins, so that the introduction of the former created a shortage of coins for small transactions, which was the reverse of the situation in the heartlands of the Frankish empire. This was particularly the case in central Italy, whose commerce had no organic link with commerce along the Po, where the situation was not so dramatic because the heavy Frankish denier was better suited to the international trade of the latter region. Nevertheless, the Frankish denier functioned in Italy more as an in-strument for the accumulation of wealth than as a means of payment. No more than 106 Carolingian coins have been found there, which is a very low figure compared to the 625 coins found in the Low Countries.

THE USE OF MONEY

The use of money, whether coined or not, or its relative scarcity, can be deduced from stipulations specifying payments for rents, for buying and selling and the like. In several cases the possibility of an alternative payment in kind or in money is indicated, even east of the Rhine where no mints existed.[9] However, statistics of the frequency of use of either of them are impossible. While there is no explicit mention

---

[8] Alessia Rovelli, 'Some Considerations on the Coinage of Lombard and Carolingian Italy', in Hansen and Wickham (eds.), *Long Eighth Century*, pp. 195–223.

[9] Dopsch, *Wirtschaftsentwicklung*, II, pp. 264–5.

in the texts of the scarcity of money, nor of dearth or shortage of victuals, wine and corn, etc. are cited as renders in kind that can be replaced by money for that reason.

An alternative case is provided by the regular replacement of renders in kind by a payment in money. The polyptych of the abbey of Prüm from the end of the ninth century (893) has several examples of this. They suggest a general tendency, which will become stronger in the tenth century. Earlier in the ninth century (829) free labour (*operarios conducere*) could be paid *in argento*, i.e. in silver, minted or not.[10] The same is true, somewhat later, even for obligatory labour services, either in agriculture or in transport. A special case is the tributes to the Danes, which may have been paid in uncoined silver.[11] Special taxes, raised for the sustenance of the poor, were levied also in uncoined silver (as at the occasion of a famine in 780). The same is true for the ban of the army (*heribannus*), which in 811 was levied in gold, silver, cloth (*palleis*), weapons and cattle.[12]

The presence and number of mints are in most cases an indication of the need for money, either because of a shortage of money or because of a flowering commerce, mostly of local importance, such as a market. The concession of a market is indeed sometimes combined with the opening of a mint, as in Rommersheim in 869, an estate of the abbey of Prüm. But normally mints are not situated in rural centres like these but in towns, either old *civitates* or younger *portus*, even if the circulation of their coins was predominantly but not exclusively local. The geographical distribution of mints and more specifically their density reveal the economically most active regions of the Frankish empire, such as the region between the Loire and the Rhine where nine-tenths of the Carolingian mints were situated. East of the Rhine there were no mints before the first one opened at Regensburg in 817. This does not mean that no coins circulated in those parts of Germany, nor that no payments were made, but that for a long time in the ninth century payments were made in kind or in uncoined silver weighed by special balances that have been discovered archaeologically in quite significant numbers.[13] The number of mints and their geographical distribution were not only dependent

---

[10] *Ibid.*, p. 270, note 5.   [11] *Ibid.*, p. 273, note 6.

[12] Boretius (ed.), *Capitularia*, I, no. 52, c.21 (AD 780); no. 166, c.2 (AD 811); no. 125, c.19 (AD 805).

[13] Heiko Steuer, 'Gewichtsgeldwirtschaften im frühgeschichtlichen Europa', in Düwel, Jankuhn *et al.*, *Untersuchungen*, IV, *Handel Karolingerzeit*, pp. 405–527.

on economic factors, but could also have political implications in one sense or another. It may reflect the king's power to control a restricted number of mints or the opposite. But still in a period of centralisation of minting, as under Charlemagne or Louis the Pious, the king never succeeded in reducing their number under ten. At best they succeeded in reducing the number of dies. After the death of Charles the Bald (877) there was a multiplication of mints conceded to bishops, especially east of the Rhine but also in France, and to abbeys.

The monetary history does not give a definite answer to the question of the role of coined money in the Carolingian economy. Therefore, it will not be surprising that the views of specialists diverge on this problem. Some of them believe that coins circulated predominantly by trade.[14] Others, in the first place one of the most eminent specialists, Philip Grierson, stated more than once that coins circulated surprisingly little and that their use in commerce was in fact of a marginal character. According to Grierson, 'they provided a standard of value and a means of storing wealth, but they did not yet play anything like the same role as a medium of exchange that coins were to do in the later Middle Ages'.[15] Metcalf has strongly contested that opinion, contending that 'early Carolingian hoards ... reveal that coinage travelled swiftly over hundreds of miles and that the velocity of circulation was sufficient'.[16] Morrison took a somewhat intermediate position, warning 'against citing Carolingian coins and coin finds as evidence of commercial relations, or the absence of numismatic remains as evidence of no commercial relations'.[17] My personal opinion is that the situation could differ from one region to another as is particularly evident when comparing the territories east and west of the Rhine or northern and central Italy. The heartlands of the Carolingian empire, that is the region between the Loire and the Rhine, being also the most densely populated and the most developed

[14] F. Vercauteren, 'Monnaie et circulation monétaire en Belgique et dans le Nord de la France du VIe au XIe siècle', in *Moneta e scambi nell'alto medioevo* (Spoleto, 1961, Settimane di studio del centro italiano di studi sull'alto medioevo, 8), pp. 279–311; D. M. Metcalf, 'The Prosperity of North-Western Europe in the Eighth and Ninth Centuries', *Economic History Review* 20 (1967), pp. 344–57.
[15] Grierson, 'Money and Coinage under Charlemagne', p. 536.
[16] Metcalf, 'Prosperity', p. 349.
[17] Karl F. Morrison, 'Numismatics and Carolingian Trade', *Speculum* 38 (1963), p. 432.

from the point of view of both rural and urban economy, were at the same time the most active and dynamic from the monetary point of view.

Much more cannot be said, especially not concerning cyclical movements of the economy on which monetary history for the Carolingian period throws no light. The only impression (and it is no more than this), is that there were ups and downs within the 150 years between the middle of the eighth and the end of the ninth century. The first ten years of the reign of Louis the Pious and the years around the edict of Pîtres (864) during the reign of Charles the Bald look economically like an upward movement. It is less than sure that the years around the reforms of Charlemagne in 793–4 were ever so prosperous, because of the famine.

PRICES

The price history of the Carolingian period is of little help in this respect because the 'supply of money' was far from being the main factor in price formation, for other means of payment, for example goods, existed. Apart from royal intervention, which is considered in Chapter 9, the free formation of prices depended primarily on supply and demand of goods. Most of the prices we know, however, were not market prices but mostly values in rentals and polyptychs that varied hardly and are of no great use. Free prices on the contrary could vary according to season. Furs for example, when their price was not fixed by a capitulary as was the case in 808,[18] were much more expensive in winter than in summer.[19] Convention between parties was also responsible for varying prices.[20]

The most sensitive prices were those of grain, bread and wine, because they depended primarily on a good or bad harvest, while bread and grain were the basic food of the population. We learn about them on the occasion of two general famines in 792–3 and 805–6

---

[18] Doehaerd, *Haut Moyen Âge*, p. 328 note 2; Boretius (ed.), *Capitularia*, I, p. 140, c.5.

[19] Dopsch, *Wirtschaftsentwicklung*, II, p. 247 note 1: '*de pellibus . . . eo quod multo carius tempore hiemis quam estatis emantur*'.

[20] Ibid., p. 248: '*prout pactio vendentis et ementis grata fuerit; quantocunque meliori precio venditor et emptor inter se dare voluerint res suas, liberam in omnibus habeant licentiam*'.

respectively that induced Charlemagne to fix maximum prices for them.[21] At the council of Frankfurt in June 794, one year after a famine that had started following the bad harvest of 792 and had continued until the new harvest of 793, Charlemagne proceeded not only to the monetary reform mentioned earlier but also, in connection with it, to a reform of weights and measures in which the newly fixed maximum prices of grain were expressed. These prices should be applied, says the text of the resolution (c.4), in times of abundance as well as in times of dearth (*sive tempore abundantiae sive tempore caritatis*). They were expressed in two ways: firstly the price of one (new) *modius* of oats, barley, rye and wheat in deniers, respectively 1, 2, 3 and 4 deniers, and secondly the number of loaves of bread, respectively of wheat, rye, barley and oats, each loaf weighing two pounds, to be purchased for one denier, namely 12, 15, 20 and 25 loaves. The latter system would be used for centuries and indicates, it may be noted in passing, that baked bread could be purchased easily by people who did not bake it themselves and were probably mostly living in towns. Perhaps to ensure the observance of these prices the king announced that if he were to sell grain from the royal stocks, an eventuality that would probably happen at particular moments of dearth, he would do it for prices half to a quarter lower than those indicated above, that is to say at a half denier for one *modius* of oats, 1 denier for barley, 2 for rye and 3 for wheat.

The prices fixed at the occasion of a new famine and this time in the midst of it, in March 806, by a famous capitulary given at Nijmegen, are, as one could expect, much higher, from 25 to 100 per cent: a *modius* of oats was now fixed at 2 deniers, barley at 3 deniers, spelt (not mentioned in 794) 3 deniers, rye 4 deniers and wheat 6 deniers. These are probably real maximum prices, fixed for that occasion, but considering that prices at later dates in the ninth century, not caused by dearth or famine, were much higher (for example, in 829 four times the prices of 806),[22] we may assume a tendency of rising prices

---

[21] Adriaan Verhulst, 'Karolingische Agrarpolitik: Das *Capitulare de Villis* und die Hungersnöte von 792/93 und 805/06', *Zeitschrift für Agrargeschichte und Agrarsoziologie* 13 (1965), pp. 175–89, reprinted in Verhulst, *Rural and Urban Aspects*, VI; Doehaerd, *Haut Moyen Âge*, pp. 58–66; Jean-Pierre Devroey, 'Units of Measurement in the Early Medieval Economy: The Example of Carolingian Food Rations', *French History* 1 (1987), pp. 68–92.

[22] Johanek, 'Fränkische Handel', p. 31, note 113.

during the first decades of the century and even later. The fixing of prices by the king was accompanied by other measures such as a prohibition of exporting victuals outside the frontiers of the empire, the controlling of the practice of selling the grain of a future harvest, the obligation for the higher classes to sustain their *familia*, that is the unfree or half-free people depending on them, before selling the surpluses of their manors, and last but not least the prohibition of usury under its different forms. The latter was a constant feature of Carolingian policy since the *Admonitio generalis* of 789.[23] It is the clearest example of the social and moral objectives of royal policy, related to the ecclesiastical doctrine of the 'just price' (*justum pretium*), which was to be developed in the course of the ninth century. The protection of the poor and Christian charity were the justification of many of the royal initiatives and interventions in economic matters; the latter were seldom the expression of an economic policy.

[23] *Ibid.*, pp. 30–1.

9

THE ECONOMY AND THE STATE

The king's interference with economic matters, however important under the Carolingians, may not straightforwardly be called an economic policy or be said to be inspired by 'semi-dirigism'.[1] For that his interventions lacked a general plan and a long term view. They were often inspired by concrete situations and were occasional and pragmatic. Let us consider different economic sectors where this opinion can be tested.

Agriculture was no doubt the most important sector and it is the one in which, more particularly, Charlemagne has been said to have practised an 'agrarian policy'.[2] This statement was based on the existence of a capitulary totally and specially devoted to the management of the royal estates and known as the capitulary *de Villis* (abbreviated *CV*).[3] Its special character, different from most capitularies containing regulations on very diverse matters, also appears from the fact that in the only existing manuscript the *CV* is preceded by three inventories of ecclesiastical and royal estates, known as the *Brevium exempla* (*BE*), clearly intended to be used as models for similar inventories.[4]

---

[1] Jean-Pierre Devroey, 'Réflexions sur l'économie des premiers temps carolingiens 768–877', *Francia* 13 (1986), pp. 475–88, reprinted in Devroey, *Grand Domaine*, no. XIV.

[2] R. Kötzschke, 'Karl der Grosse als Agrarpolitiker', in *Festschrift Edmund Stengel* (1952), pp. 181–94.

[3] Carlrichard Brühl (ed.), *Capitulare de Villis* (Stuttgart, 1971: Dokumente zur deutschen Geschichte in Faksimiles, I,1); Boretius (ed.), *Capitularia*, no. 32.

[4] Boretius (ed.), *Capitularia*, no. 128; see Chapter 3, pp. 32–3, 39–40.

The long format of the manuscript (29.5 to 12.5 cm) suggests that it had actually been used on inspection tours as a model. While the manuscript probably dates from around 825, the date of the text itself of the *CV* can approximately be placed between 792–3 and 800. The text, without much logical order, was probably drawn up in the aftermath of the famine of 792–3.[5] Its main concern is the supply of the army and the court, especially during military campaigns. Several articles (c. 30, 33, 64, 68) refer to it. The link between *CV* and *BE* is not purely coincidental, for the impact of some articles of *CV* upon *BE* is clear, for example in the enumeration of artisans to be present on the estates, which is similar in both documents. Some passages in *BE*, originally containing placenames and figures of volumes of grain stocks, have a formulary form (replaced by *ille*, *tantus*, etc.), that is however far from complete. An expression like *et sic de ceteris numerabis* (you will number further in this way) has been evidently inserted with the intention that *BE* function as a model.[6] Whether such particularities are of 'private' or 'official' origin is difficult to say and the same is true for the whole *BE*. What is highly probable however is that the copyist or compiler did find in the chancery the inventories he put together to form *BE*. Indeed, the court wanted to be informed on the potentialities of ecclesiastical and royal estates – grain production, cattle, peasant farms (*mansi*), vassals, etc. – mainly for the supply of the army but also for other reasons such as their concession to important members of the aristocracy, the collection of tributes to the Norsemen or on the occasion of political divisions of territories and even of the empire. Many traces of orders and instructions in that sense have been preserved and even fragments of inventories that correspond to what was expected. Such inventories, consisting only of a summing up of the number of *mansi*, of inhabitants, cattle, stocks, etc., must be distinguished from polyptychs, which essentially contain detailed data on the rents, deliveries and services to which the different categories of inhabitants of the estate, whose names are often given, were obliged. As proprietor of the royal estates the king might have been interested in polyptychs of the latter, but as head of the empire he needed inventories both of his own estates and of those of the church and the aristocracy. The function of inventories and polyptychs was not only different from

[5] Verhulst, '*Capitulare de Villis*'.
[6] Verhein, 'Quellen zum Reichsgut', pp. 348–52.

each other, but the latter may not always have been drawn up by royal order. Devroey has indeed made clear, taking his examples from the church of Rheims, that archbishops, bishops and abbots, as managers of their estates, have contributed to the development of estate surveys which in the ninth century reached their classic form of polyptychs and how this development was directly linked to the instauration of the classical bipartite exploitation regime of big estates.[7] Devroey, however, has gone too far claiming that 'the Carolingian *villa* was a voluntaristic economic model, being at the same time instrument and reflection of a coherent political idea'.[8] I do not doubt that the building up of the manorial regime, since the seventh century, was favoured by the Merovingian and Carolingian rulers in order to reach the highest agricultural production through the best possible management and the application of instructions such as those given in the *CV*, but it would be an exaggeration to consider their efforts as the expression of what would be called an 'agrarian policy'. Even an important document in that respect, such as the *CV*, was not the systematic statement of such a policy, but a very unsystematic collection of practical instructions, drawn up under the impression of a recent famine.

The measures taken by the king on the occasion of famines or dearths can also hardly be considered the expression of an agrarian policy. In a first phase some measures prescribed by the king were purely religious, ordering the clergy to read masses and say prayers and imposing fasting on everyone. Other instructions inspired by charity prescribed the feeding of the poor and of those who suffered. More particularly the proprietors and holders of estates and fiefs (*beneficia*) were ordered to provide for the *familia* living on them, perhaps not so much out of charity but with the aim of keeping up the economic capacity of these estates. In a second phase of the famine the preserving of the royal manors, their production capacity and their stocks were the main concern. At the same time building up of grain stocks with speculative intentions, for example by purchasing future harvests, and other practices of usury were strictly prohibited. Finally maximum grain prices and weight and prices of bread were fixed, on the occasion of the famines of 792–3 and 806, as we have seen in Chapter 8.

[7] Jean-Pierre Devroey, 'Les premiers polyptyques rémois, VIIe-IXe siècles', in Verhulst (ed.), *Grand domaine*, pp. 78–97, reprinted in Devroey, *Grand domaine*, no. II.
[8] Devroey, 'Réflexions', p. 478.

Because of their more systematic character and their monetary aspects these measures may be considered part of what might be called an 'economic policy' for the short term. They come near to a monetary policy and were on some occasions part of it, like at the council of Frankfurt 794 in the aftermath of the famine of 792–3. The dealing with monetary problems by the successive Carolingian rulers since Pipin III has many aspects indeed of a systematic and comprehensive policy for the long term. Many capitularies have articles on monetary problems and a few are totally or for a large part devoted to them. As such these offer evidence of the constant care of the Carolingians for good and stable money and for monetary unity over the whole empire, their fight against counterfeiting, their solicitude for measures accompanying the introduction of new coins (turning in of old coins, decoinage, stringent penalties for those who did not accept and rejected new coins) and their attitude towards foreign coins, which were systematically melted. The enforcement of some aspects of this policy did not always produce the expected results, as was the case for instance with the efforts to centralise minting on one or a strictly limited number of places.

The fundamental aim of the different aspects of Carolingian monetary policy was political: good money, uniformly accepted over the whole empire, was in the first place a question of prestige. Fiscal profits from minting new coins were no doubt real but were not, as such, an objective, in contrast to so many rulers of the late Middle Ages. Economic motives may be detected in some rare cases where a market was founded by the Carolingian king together with the opening of a mint. This would become a systematic policy of the Ottonians east of the Rhine in the tenth century. In the ninth century the number of markets had increased without royal intervention but it leaves no doubt that the king was eager to provide money for their functioning.

The flowering of markets during the ninth century was certainly not the result of any direct intervention by the king inspired by a policy in matters of trade and commerce. This does not mean that markets were not the king's concern. He 'legalised' markets, controlled their number and existence, and in order to fight the evading of market tolls, ordered that all business should be done on a 'legal' market. Charles the Bald thus authorised nineteen markets, fifteen in the second half of his reign. Janet Nelson, on the basis of Charles's Edict of Pîtres (864), thinks that his determination to keep control of markets was for political and fiscal motives.[9] The issuing of authorisations was surely profitable indeed.

The attitude of the Carolingian kings towards tolls cannot without difficulty be considered the expression of a policy. Therefore the opinions of two modern specialists of these matters, Mitterauer and Adam, actually differ too strongly on that point, the latter author arguing that tolls, and particularly toll exemptions, were an instrument of Carolingian trade policy, while the former denies them any economic significance.[10] Without being as radical as these authors, two points at least in the attitude of Carolingian kings towards tolls may be interpreted as signs of their active intervention in trade, positively and negatively. On the positive side, the Carolingian kings reacted to the multiplication of tolls during the ninth century, ordering that a distinction be made between 'old' and 'new' tolls, the latter being qualified 'unjust' in the well-known capitulary of Thionville (805).[11] Rather unfavourable to commerce was their concern with the frontiers of the empire, whether in the *emporia* on the North Sea and Channel coast, where even royal merchants had to pay the 10 per cent tax, or at the Alpine passes and in the border region with the Avars. We can assume that at these frontier posts, and also on the Elbe, trade, especially the export of weapons, was severely controlled. Importation however, for example along the Danube, upstream from the Avar frontier, well known from the famous Raffelstetten inquiry, was favoured by lower toll tariffs, as was explained in Chapter 7. *Emporia*, as was also explained earlier, more specifically Quentovic and Dorestad, were administered by a special royal agent (*procurator, prefectus emporii*), who had the supervision over old *civitates* in their neighbourhood like Rouen and Amiens.

The *Praeceptum negotiatorum* of Louis the Pious (828) is a collection of instructions for the 'merchants of the palace', who were on a permanent and private basis trading for the king.[12] For that reason the document cannot be used in a general way as evidence for the king's intervention in trade, although, as these merchants traded at the same time for themselves, their privileges as merchants of the king must have been to the profit of trade in general. The same

---

[9] Janet L. Nelson, *Charles the Bald*, pp. 30–1.
[10] Adam, *Zollwesen*, p. 239.   [11] *Ibid.*, pp. 223–4.
[12] K. Zeumer (ed.), *Formulae merovingici et karolini aevi* (Hanover, 1886; MGH, LL, v), no. 37; François-L.Ganshof, 'Note sur le "Praeceptum Negotiatorum" de Louis le Pieux', in *Studi in onore di A. Sapori*, I (1957), pp. 101–12.

must have been true for Jewish merchants, who were in the same position, although Jewish merchants in general too were particularly well protected by the king throughout the empire because of their importance especially for foreign trade.[13]

Finally the king's concern for infrastructure – bridges, roads, fares, etc. – many times the object of royal orders for repair and maintenance in the capitularies, may in the first place have had military reasons, although it benefited trade.

[13] C. Verlinden, 'A propos de la place des Juifs dans l'économie de l'Europe occiden-tale aux ixe et xe siècles', in *Storiografia e storia. Studi in onore di Eugenio Dupré Theseider*, vol. i (Rome, 1974), pp. 21–37.

10

THE LONG PERSPECTIVE

———— • ————

The place of the Carolingian age and more particularly of the Carolingian economy in the history of the early Middle Ages, between late Antiquity and the expansion of the European economy from the eleventh to the thirteenth centuries, has for a long time been the object of much debate. Since the publication of two books by Alfons Dopsch between 1918 and 1921, respectively on the transition of Antiquity to the Middle Ages[1] and the economy of the Carolingian period,[2] and of two articles by Henri Pirenne, in 1922 and 1923, on the economic contrast between Merovingians and Carolingians,[3] and a posthumous book in 1937, well known under its title *Mahomet et Charlemagne*,[4] there has been discussion around the question of whether the Carolingian age was a period of economic revival as contrasted with the preceding centuries, as Dopsch

---

[1] Alfons Dopsch, *Wirtschaftliche und soziale Grundlagen der europäischen Kulturentwicklung aus der Zeit von Cäsar bis auf Karl den Grossen*, 2 vols., second edition (Vienna, 1923–4), abridged translation: *The Economic and Social Foundations of European Civilisation* (London, 1937).

[2] Dopsch, *Wirtschaftsentwicklung*.

[3] Henri Pirenne, 'Mahomet et Charlemagne', *Revue belge de philologie et d'histoire* 1(1922), pp. 77–86; 'Un contraste économique: Mérovingiens et Carolingiens', *Revue belge de philologie et d'histoire* 2 (1923), pp. 223–35.

[4] Henri Pirenne, *Mohammed and Charlemagne*, English translation (London, Irwin, 1939); paperback edition by Barnes and Noble (New York, 1955).

contended, or, as Pirenne argued, an economic nadir, a self-sufficient agrarian economy without towns or trade.[5]

Neither author, like many others participating in the debate, paid much attention to possible cyclical movements within the period itself. Understandable though this is, given the scarce indications from the sources in this respect, an enquiry into possible sub-periods is nevertheless a step towards a more nuanced approach of the period as a whole.

Towns and trade probably are the best variables to detect cyclical movements with which other aspects of economic life can be linked. Not only has the discussion been mostly centred around them, but documentary evidence about them can be combined with archaeological and numismatic data.

In north-west Europe, in the regions around the North Sea in which even Pirenne admitted, be it only very temporary, signs of urban life, the end of the seventh century was marked by the beginnings of non-agricultural settlements, the population of which was predominantly composed of craftsmen, merchants and boaters. Richard Hodges has called them '*emporia* B', because they were no longer, as the '*emporia* A' had been at the beginning of the century, ephemeral places of mainly gift-exchange for an elite, but real towns with an urban lay-out, like a grid of streets, an artisanal production and regional and long-distance trade.[6] Dorestad on the Rhine in present-day Holland is the best known of them. What interests us now, since the functions of these towns have already been described, is their chronology. The first half of the eighth century, the age of Charles Martel, is a dark moment in this chronology, because of unrest and military expeditions. It may be characterised as the gap between Merovingian and Carolingian times, although archaeology sees a continuous development of these '*emporia* B' through that period. However, the hey-day of Dorestad and similar towns, also its numismatic peak, was from 775–80 to 825. During these years Charlemagne in 793–4 and Louis the Pious in 818 had upgraded the penny respectively to 1.7 g and 1.8 g, the latter bringing it back to 1.7 g in 822–3. This coincidence may be significant and could be interpreted as a sign of economic prosperity. The famines of the same

[5] Bryce D. Lyon, *The Origins of the Middle Ages. Pirenne's Challenge to Gibbon* (New York, 1972).
[6] Hodges, *Towns and Trade*.

period, in 779, 792–3 and 805–6, apparently had no impact on that upward movement and may rather be explained by the population pressure of those years of which there are indications, such as the demographic data in the polyptych of St Victor of Marseilles at the beginning of the ninth century and the overpopulation and small size of the *mansi* in the Paris region in the polyptych of abbot Irmino around 825. After 825–30 the '*emporia* B' declined and a period of political unrest and even military operations began with the revolt of Lothar against Louis the Pious in 833–4 and the struggles between the latter's sons, which ended with the treaty of Verdun in 843. The first Viking attacks, on Dorestad in 835 and 837, on Antwerp and *Witla* in 836, and the enfeoffment to the Danish leaders of Walcheren (with the *emporium* of Domburg) in 841 and of Dorestad in 850, were not without links to the political situation.[7] A second wave of Viking attacks in the 840s and 850s infested nearly year after year the rivermouths of north-west France and Flanders. At the mouth of the Canche river, Quentovic was attacked in 842, while several years between 841 and 865 at the mouth of the Seine, and between 853 and 872 at the mouth of the Loire, the Vikings only retreated because of the heavy tributes paid by Charles the Bald from the royal treasury, from churches and from taxes on landholders, not without negative consequences for the silver content of the penny. Once more and for the last time Dorestad was sacked in 863. The tide turned in the early 860s, when defences were built that successfully beat off new attacks, as did the stronghold of Bruges in 864. Meanwhile new towns or new or revived commercial centres in old towns, described as *portus* in documentary sources and on coins, had taken the place of the *emporia* which around the middle of the ninth century had nearly all disappeared. Valenciennes, Tournai and Ghent on the Scheldt river, Maastricht, Huy and Dinant on the Meuse are well-known examples of this new type of town, situated on the rivers inland, the commercial range of which was more limited than that of the *emporia* and for a long time more regional. Their appearance around the middle of the ninth century is an indication of a new period of prosperity that lasted only some decades before a new wave of Viking attacks began in 879. This time most new towns survived, some however, like Valenciennes and Ghent not without a break of some twenty to thirty years. The famous edict of Pîtres, which Charles the Bald

[7] Simon Coupland, 'The Vikings in Francia and Anglo-Saxon England to 911', in *The New Cambridge Medieval History* (Cambridge, 1995), II, pp. 190–201.

issued in 864 also testifies to this revival, especially its long articles on the restoration of money, its interest for markets and its exhortations for the building of defences.[8]

That economic movements like those we believe to have detected in north-west Europe, the heartlands of the Carolingians, were not purely regional is demonstrated by the evolution of urban life in Italy. After places like Brescia, Naples, Milan, Otranto and Pescara had been reduced to non-urban proportions in the seventh and eighth centuries, a revival, especially of Venice and Rome, occurred in the ninth century. From the later eighth century, between 774 and 860, especially under the papacies of Hadrian I and Leo III (772–95 and 795–816), a real renaissance in Rome refurbished many churches and built new ones.[9]

Considering the eighth and ninth centuries as a whole, it is clear that with the exception of the first half of the eighth century, which economically remains a problem, given the existence of *emporia* type B from the end of the seventh century onwards, the years 775–90 to 830 and 850–60 to 879, were particularly flourishing. A decline, however, is clearly visible and universally agreed between *c.* 830 and *c.* 850, for which political unrest and Viking attacks are generally held responsible. The flourishing during half a century around the year 800 coincides with a summit in the organisation and exploitation of big estates, producing a surplus in those years that even then was not sufficient to prevent famines and dearths. The second upheaval, during a pause in the Viking attacks in the 860s, was apparently and in the first place commercial and marked by the beginning of new towns. Still a point of discussion is the question of whether this flowering of trade was in some way or another the effect of the presence of Vikings, whose attacks were not always so devastating as clerical sources make us believe. It finally depends on our judgment of the seventh century if we may call the Carolingian age as a whole a time of economic revival and on our views on the difficult tenth century if we believe that this revival was only temporary, without longlasting effects. The latter is not my opinion for I see the Carolingian period as part of a nearly continuous upward movement from the seventh century onwards, at least as far as the northern half of Carolingian Europe is concerned.

---

[8] Nelson, *Charles the Bald*, pp. 30–40.
[9] Hansen and Wickham (eds.), *Long Eighth Century*, pp. 358–63; Hodges, *Towns and Trade*, pp. 99–101.

BIBLIOGRAPHY

———————— • ————————

PRIMARY SOURCES

Boretius, A. (ed.), *Capitularia regum Francorum*, 2 vols., Hanover, 1883; reprint 1984.

Brühl, Carlrichard (ed.), *Capitulare de Villis*, Stuttgart, 1971 (Dokumente zur deutschen Geschichte in Faksimiles, 1,1).

Dette, Christoph (ed.), *Liber possessionum Wizenburgensis*, Mainz, 1987.

Devroey, Jean-Pierre (ed.), *Le polyptyque et les listes de cens de l'abbaye de Saint-Remi de Reims (IXe–XIe siècles)*, Reims, 1984.

  (ed.), *Le polyptyque et les listes de biens de l'abbbaye Saint-Pierre de Lobbes (IXe–XIe siècles)*, Brussels, 1986.

Droste, Claus-Dieter (ed.), *Das Polytichon von Montierender*, Trier, 1988.

Ganshof, François-L. (ed.), *Le Polyptyque de l'abbaye de Saint-Bertin (844–859)*, Paris, 1975.

Guérard, Benjamin, Delisle, Léopold and Marion, A., *Cartulaire de l'abbaye de Saint-Victor de Marseille*, Paris, 1857.

Gysseling, Maurits and Koch, Anton (eds.), *Diplomata belgica ante annum millesimum centesimum scripta*, Tongeren, 1950.

Hägermann, Dieter, Elmshäuser, Konrad and Hedwig, Andreas (eds.), *Das Polyptychon von Saint-Germain-des-Prés*, Cologne, Weimar, Vienna, 1993.

Hägermann, Dieter and Hedwig, Andreas (eds.), *Das Polyptychon und die Notitia de Areis von Saint-Maur-des-Fossés*, Sigmaringen, 1989.

Loyn, H. R. and Percival, John, *The Reign of Charlemagne. Documents on Carolingian Government and Administration*, London, 1975.

Niermeyer, J. F., *Mediae Latiniatis Lexicon Minus*, Leiden, 1976.

Ogg, Frederic A (ed.), *A Sourcebook of Mediaeval History*, New York, 1907; reprint 1972, part of *Internet Medieval Sourcebook*, ed. P. Halsall, 1988.

Schwab, Ingo (ed.), *Das Prümer Urbar*, Düsseldorf, 1983.

Schwind, E. von (ed.), *Leges* 5, 2 Hanover, 1926 (MGH, LL, V).

Tessier, Georges (ed.), *Recueil des actes de Charles II le Chauve, roi de France*, 3 vols., Paris, 1943–55.

Zeumer, K. (ed.), *Formulae merovingici et karolini aevi*, Hanover, 1886 (MGH, LL, V).

SECONDARY WORKS

Abbé, Jean-Loup, 'Permanences et mutations des parcellaires médiévaux', in Chouquer, G. (ed.), *Les formes du paysage*, vol. II, *Archéologie des parcellaires*, Paris, 1996, pp. 223–33.

Adam, Hildegard, *Das Zollwesen im fränkischen Reich und seine Bedeutung für das spätkarolingische Wirtschaftsleben*, Stuttgart, 1996.

Adelson, H. L., 'Early Medieval Trade Routes', *American Historical Review* 65 (1960), pp. 271–87.

Agache, R., *La Somme pré-romaine et romaine*, Amiens, 1978 (Mémoires de la Société des Antiquaires de Picardie, in-4° series, 24).

Alberts, W. J. and Jansen, H. P. H., *Welvaart in Wording. Sociaal-economische geschiedenis van Nederland van de vroegste tijden tot het einde van de Middeleeuwen*, The Hague, 1964.

Ambrosiani, Björn, 'Excavations in the Black Earth Harbour 1969–71', in Ambrosiani, Björn and Clarke, Helen (eds.), *Early Investigations and Future Plans*, Stockholm, 1992 (Birka Studies 1).

Andreolli, Bruno and Montanari, Massimo, *L'aziende curtense in Italia*, Bologna, 1985.

Astill, Grenville and Langdon, John, *Medieval Farming and Technology. The Impact of Agricultural Change in Northwest Europe*, Leiden, 1997.

Beck, Heinrich, Denecke, Dietrich and Jankuhn, Herbert (eds.), *Untersuchungen zur eisenzeitlichen und frühmittelalterlichen Flur in Mitteleuropa und ihrer Nutzung*, 2 vols., Göttingen, 1979–80 (Abhandlungen der Akademie der Wissenschaften, Phil.-Histor. Klasse, 3rd series, 115–16).

Bessmerny, J. 'Les structures de la famille paysanne dans les villages de la Francia au IXe siècle', *Le Moyen Age* 90 (1984), pp. 165–93.

Besteman J. C., Bos J. M. and Heidinga H. A. (eds.), *Medieval Archaeology in the Netherlands. Studies presented to H. H. van Regteren Altena*, Assen and Maastricht, 1990.

Bloch, Marc, 'Avènement et conquêtes du moulin à l'eau', *Annales d'Histoire Economique et Sociale* 7 (1935), pp. 538–63.

Bolin, Sture, 'Mohammad, Charlemagne and Ruric', *Scandinavian Economic History Review* 1 (1953), pp. 5–39.

Bonnassie, Pierre, 'La croissance agricole du haut moyen âge dans la Gaule du Midi et le Nord-Est de la péninsule ibérique', in *La croissance agricole*, Auch 1990, pp. 13–35 (Flaran 10).

   La Catalogne autour de l'an mil, second edition, 2 vols., Paris, 1990.

Bourin, Monique, 'Délimitation des parcelles et perception de l'espace en Bas-Languedoc aux xe et xie siècles', in *Campagnes médiévales: l'homme et son espace. Etudes offertes à Robert Fossier*, Paris, 1995.

Braunfels, Wolfgang, Beumann, Helmut, Schnitzler, Hermann and Bischoff, Bernhard (eds.), *Karl der Grosse. Lebenswerk und Nachleben*, 4 vols., Düsseldorf, 1965.

Burguière, André, Klapisch-Zuber, Christiane *et al.* (eds.), *Histoire de la famille*, 2 vols., Paris, 1986.

Castagnetti, A., Luzatti, M., Pasquali, G. and Vasina, A. (eds.), *Inventari altomedievali di terre, coloni e redditi*, Rome, 1979 (Fonti per la Storia d'Italia 104).

Champion, Etienne, *Moulins et meuniers carolingiens dans les polyptyques entre Loire et Rhin*, Paris, 1996.

Chapelot, Jean and Fossier, Robert, *Le village et la maison au moyen âge*, Paris, 1980.

Chédeville, André and Tonnerre, Noël-Yves, *La Bretagne féodale XIe–XIIIe siècle*, Rennes, 1987.

Chouquer, Gérard (ed.), *Les formes du paysage*, 3 vols., Paris, 1996.

   'Parcellaires et longue durée', in Chouquer (ed.), *Les formes du paysage*, vol. II, *Archéologie des parcellaires*, pp. 213–18.

Christie, N. and Loseby, S. T. (eds.), *Towns in Transition: Urban Evolution in Late Antiquity and the Early Middle Ages*, Aldershot, 1996.

Clarke, Helen and Ambrosiani, Björn, *Towns in the Viking Age*, second revised edition, London, Leicester University Press, 1995.

Claude, Dietrich, *Der Handel im westlichen Mittelmeer während des Frühmittelalters*, Göttingen, 1985. (Düwel *et al.* (eds.), *Untersuchungen zu Handel und Verkehr der vor- und frühgeschichtlichen Zeit in Mittel- und Nordeuropa*, vol. 2 = Abhandlungen Akademie Göttingen, Phil.-Hist. Klasse, 3rd series, no. 144).

Clavadetscher, Otto P., 'Zum churrätischen Reichsguturbar aus der Karolingerzeit', *Zeitschrift für schweizerische Geschichte* 30 (1950), pp. 161–97.

Clemens, L. and Matheus, M., 'Zur Keltertechnik in karolingischer Zeit', in *Liber Amicorum für A. Heit* (1995), pp. 255–65.

Comet, Georges, 'Technology and Agricultural Expansion in the Middle Ages: The Example of France North of the Loire', in Astill, Grenville and Langdon, John (eds.), *Medieval Farming and Technology*, Leiden, 1997, pp. 11–39.

Corbet, Patrick (ed.), *Les moines du Der 673–1790*, Langres, 2000.

Coupland, Simon, 'Money and Coinage under Louis the Pious', *Francia* 17 (1990), pp. 23–54.

'The Early Coinage of Charles the Bald', *Numismatic Chronicle* 151 (1991), pp. 121–58.

'The Vikings in Francia and Anglo-Saxon England to 911', in *The New Cambridge Medieval History*, Cambridge, 1995, II, pp. 190–201.

'The Frankish Tribute Payments to the Vikings and their Consequences', *Francia* 26 (1999), pp. 57–75.

La croissance agricole du Haut Moyen Age. Chronologie, modalités, géographie, Auch, 1990 (Flaran 10, 1988).

Cuisenier, Jean and Guadagnin, Rémy (eds.), *Un village au temps de Charlemagne*, Paris, 1988.

Dekker, Cornelis, *Zuid-Beveland. De historische geografie en de instellingen van een Zeeuws eiland in de Middeleeuwen*, Assen, 1971.

Delogu, Paolo, 'Reading Pirenne Again', in Hodges, Richard and Bowden, William (eds.), *The Sixth Century. Production, Distribution and Demand*, Leiden, Brill, 1998, pp. 15–40.

Dept, Gaston G., 'Le mot *clusas* dans les diplômes carolingiens', in *Mélanges d'Histoire offerts à Henri Pirenne*, I, Brussels, 1926, pp. 89–98.

Derville, Alain, 'Le marais de Saint-Omer', *Revue du Nord* 62 (1980), pp. 73–95, reprinted in Derville, Alain, *Douze études d'histoire rurale. Flandre, Artois, Cambrésis au moyen âge*, Lille, 1996, pp. 67–88.

Despy, Georges, 'Villes et campagnes aux IXe et Xe siècles: l'exemple du pays mosan', *Revue du Nord* 50 (1968), pp. 145–68.

Devroey, Jean-Pierre, '*Mansi absi*: indices de crise ou de croissance de l'économie rurale du haut moyen âge', *Le Moyen Age* 82 (1976), pp. 421–51, reprinted in Devroey, *Grand domaine*, no. IX.

'A propos d'un article récent: l'utilisation du polyptyque d'Irminon en démographie', *Revue belge de philologie et d'histoire* 55 (1977), pp. 509–14; reprinted in Devroey, *Grand domaine* no. IV.

'Les services de transport à l'abbaye de Prüm au IXe siècle', *Revue du Nord* 61 (1979), pp. 543–69, reprinted in Devroey, *Grand domaine* no. X.

'Les méthodes d'analyse démographique des polyptyques du haut moyen âge', *Acta Historica Bruxellensia* 4 (1981), pp. 71–88, reprinted in Devroey, *Grand domaine*, no. V.

'Un monastère dans l'économie d'échanges: les services de transport à l'abbaye de Saint-Germain-des-Prés au IXe siècle', *Annales. Economies–Sociétés–Civilisations* (1984), pp. 570–89, reprinted in Devroey, *Grand Domaine* no. XI.

'Les premiers polyptyques rémois, VIIe–IXe siècles', in Verhulst (ed.), *Grand domaine*, pp. 78–97, reprinted in Devroey, *Grand domaine*, no. II.

'Réflexions sur l'économie des premiers temps carolingiens (768–877)', *Francia* 13 (1986), pp. 475–88, reprinted in Devroey, *Grand domaine*, no. XIV.

'Units of Measurement in the Early Medieval Economy: The Example of Carolingian Food Rations', *French History* 1 (1987), pp. 68–92.

'Entre Loire et Rhin: les fluctuations du terroir de l'épeautre au moyen âge', in Devroey and Van Mol (eds.), *L'épeautre*, pp. 89–105, reprinted in Devroey, *Grand domaine*, no. VII.

'La céréaliculture dans le monde franc', in *L'ambiente vegetale nell'alto medioevo*, Spoleto, 1990 (Settimane di studio 37), pp. 221–53, reprinted in Devroey, *Grand domaine*, no. VI.

'Courants et réseaux d'échange dans l'économie franque entre Loire et Rhin', in *Mercati e Mercanti nell'alto medioevo*, Spoleto, 1993 (Settimane di studio 40).

Etudes sur le grand domaine carolingien, Aldershot, 1993 (Variorum).

Devroey J.-P. and Van Mol, J.-J. (eds.), *L'épeautre (Triticum spelta), histoire et ethnologie*, Treignes, 1989.

Doehaerd, Renée, 'Les réformes monétaires carolingiennes', *Annales. Economies-Sociétés-Civilisations* 7 (1952), pp. 13–20, reprinted in Doehaerd, *Oeconomica Mediaevalia*, pp. 149–57.

Le Haut Moyen Âge Occidental. Economie et sociétés, Paris, 1971. Transl. *Early Middle Ages in the West. Economy and Society*, New York, 1978.

Oeconomica Mediaevalia, Brussels, 1984.

Dopsch, Alfons, *Die Wirtschaftsentwicklung der Karolingerzeit vornehmlich in Deutschland*, second revised edition, 2 vols.,Weimar, 1921–2.

Wirtschaftliche und soziale Grundlagen der europäischen Kulturentwicklung aus der Zeit von Cäsar bis auf Karl den Grossen, 2 vols., 2nd edition, Vienna, 1923–4. Abridged translation: *The Economic and Social Foundations of European Civilisation*, London, 1937.

Droste, Claus-Dieter, 'Die Grundherrschaft Montiérender im 9. Jahrhundert', in Verhulst (ed.), *Grand domaine*, pp. 101–11.

Duby, Georges, *L'économie rurale et la vie des campagnes dans l'Occident médiéval*, Paris, 1962. Transl. *Rural Economy and Country Life in the Medieval West*, Los Angeles, 1968.

'Le problème des techniques agricoles', in *Agricoltura e mondo rurale in Occidente nell'alto medioevo*, Spoleto, 1966, pp. 267–83.

The Early Growth of the European Economy. Warriors and Peasants from the Seventh to the Twelfth Century, Ithaca, 1978 (Cornell University Press).

Duparc, P., 'Les cluses et la frontière des Alpes', *Bibliothèque de l'Ecole des Chartes* 109 (1951), pp. 5–31.

Durliat, J., *Les finances publiques de Dioclétien aux Carolingiens (284–889)*, Sigmaringen, 1990 (Beihefte der Francia 21).

Düwel, Klaus, Jankuhn, Herbert, Siems, Harald and Timpe, Dieter (eds.), *Untersuchungen zu Handel und Verkehr der vor- und frühgeschichtlichen Zeit in Mittel- und Nord-Europa*, 6 vols., Göttingen, 1985–9 (Abhandlungen der Akademie der Wissenschaften, Philol.-Histor. Klasse, 3rd series, nos. 143, 144, 150, 156, 180, 183).

Elmshäuser, Konrad, 'Untersuchungen zum Staffelseer Urbar', in Rösener (ed.), *Strukturen der Grundherrschaft*, pp. 335–69.

Elmshäuser, Konrad and Hedwig, Andreas, *Studien zum Polyptychon von Saint-Germain-des-Prés*, Cologne, Weimar, Vienna, 1993.

Feller, L., Mane, P. and Piponnier, F. (eds.), *Le village médiéval et son environnement. Etudes offertes à Jean-Marie Pesez*, Paris, 1998.

Fenske, L., Rösener, W. and Zotz, Th. (eds.), *Institutionen, Kultur und Gesellschaft im Mittelalter. Festschrift für Josef Fleckenstein*, Sigmaringen, 1984.

Fossier, Robert, 'Les tendances de l'économie: stagnation ou croissance?', in *Nascita dell'Europa ed Europa Carolingia*, Spoleto, 1981 (Settimane di Studio del Centro italiano di studi sull'alto medioevo 27), pp. 261–74.

Fournier, Gabriel, *Le peuplement rural en Basse Auvergne durant le haut moyen âge*, Paris, 1962.

Ganshof, François-L., 'Note sur les ports de Provence du VIIIe au xe siècle', *Revue Historique* 183 (1938), pp. 28–37.

'Note sur le "Praeceptum Negotiatorum" de Louis le Pieux', in *Studi in onore di A. Sapori*, I (1957), pp. 101–12.

'L'étranger dans la monarchie franque', *Recueils Société Jean Bodin* 10, 2 (1958), pp. 5–36.

Frankish Institutions under Charlemagne, New York, 1970 (Norton Library).

'A propos du tonlieu à l'époque carolingienne', in *La città nell'alto medioevo*, Spoleto, 1959 (Settimane di studi del Centro italiano di studi sull'alto medioevo, 6), pp. 485–508.

'Note sur l' "Inquisitio de theloneis Raffelstettensis"', *Le Moyen Âge* 72 (1966), pp. 197–224.

'Das Fränkische Reich', in Kellenbenz (ed.), *Handbuch der europäischen Wirtschafts- und Sozialgeschichte*, vol. II, pp. 151–205.

La genèse et les premiers siècles des villes médiévales dans les Pays-Bas méridionaux. Un problème archéologique et historique, Brussels, 1990 (Crédit Communal, coll. Histoire in-8°, no. 83).

Gibson, M. T. and Nelson, J. L., *Charles the Bald. Court and Kingdom*, second revised edition, London, 1990.

Goetz, Hans-Werner, 'Herrschaft und Raum inder frühmittelalterlichen Grundherrschaft', *Annalen des Historischen Vereins für den Niederrhein* 190 (1987), pp. 7–33.

'Social and Military Institutions', in McKitterick (ed.), *The New Cambridge Medieval History*, vol. II, pp. 451–80.

Grierson, Philip, 'Carolingian Europe and the Arabs: The Myth of the
    Mancus', *Revue belge de philologie et d'histoire* 32 (1954), pp. 1059–74.
'Commerce in the Dark Ages: A Critique of the Evidence', *Transactions
    of the Royal Historical Society*, 5th Series 9 (1959), pp. 123–40, reprinted
    in Grierson Philip, *Dark Age Numismatics*, London, 1979.
'The Monetary Reforms of Abd-Al-Malik', *Journal of Economic and Social
    History of the Orient*, 3 (1960), pp. 241–64.
'Money and Coinage under Charlemagne', in Braunfels *et al.* (eds.), *Karl
    der Grosse*, I, pp. 501–36, reprinted in Grierson, *Dark Age Numismatics*,
    no. XVIII.
Dark Age Numismatics, London, 1979.
'The *Gratia Dei Rex* Coinage of Charles the Bald', in Gibson and Nelson
    (eds.), *Charles the Bald. Court and Kingdom*, pp. 52–64.
Grierson, Philip and Blackburn, Mark, *Medieval European Coinage: With a
    Catalogue of the Coins in the Fitzwilliam Museum Cambridge*, 10 vols., I:
    The Early Middle Ages (Fifth–Tenth Centuries), Cambridge, New York,
    1986.
Guerreau, Alain, 'L'évolution du parcellaire en Mâconnais (env. 900–env.
    1060)' in Feller, Mane and Piponnier (eds.), *Le village médiéval et son
    environnement*, pp. 509–35.
Hägermann, Dieter, 'Einige Aspekte der Grundherrschaft in den fränkischen
    formulae und in den leges des Frühmittelalters', in Verhulst (ed.), *Grand
    domaine*, pp. 51–77.
Hägermann, Dieter and Schneider, Helmuth, *Landbau und Handwerk 750 v.
    Chr. Bis 1000 n. Chr.*, Berlin, 1991 (König, Wolfgang (ed.), *Propyläen
    Technikgeschichte*).
Hall, R. A., 'The Decline of the Wic?' in Slater (ed.), *Towns in Decline*,
    pp. 120–36.
Hansen, I. L. and Wickham, C. (eds.), *The Long Eighth Century*, Leiden, 2000.
Higounet, Charles, 'Les forêts de l'Europe occidentale du Ve au XIe siècle',
    in *Agricoltura e mondo rurale in Occidente nell'alto medioevo*, Spoleto, 1966
    (Settimane di studio del Centro italiano di studi sull'alto medioevo 13),
    pp. 343–98.
Hildebrandt, H., 'Systems of Agriculture in Central Europe up to the
    Tenth and Eleventh Centuries', in Hooke, Della (ed.), *Anglo-Saxon
    Settlements*, Oxford, 1988, pp. 81–101.
Hodges, Richard, *Dark Age Economics. The Origins of Towns and Trade AD
    600–1000*, London, 1982.
    Light in the Dark Ages. The Rise and Fall of San Vincenzo al Volturno, London,
    1997.
    Towns and Trade in the Age of Charlemagne, London, 2000.
Hodges, Richard and Hobley, Brian (eds.), *The Rebirth of Towns in the West
    AD 700–1050*, London, 1988 (CBA Research Report 68).

Hodges, Richard and Whitehouse, David, *Mohammed, Charlemagne and the Origins of Europe*, London, 1983.

Horn, W. and Born, E., *The Plan of St Gall*, 3 vols., University of California Press, Berkeley, Los Angeles, 1979.

Hubert, Jean, 'La renaissance carolingienne et la topographie religieuse des cités épiscopales', in *I problemi della civiltà carolingia*, Spoleto, 1954 (Settimane di studio del Centro italiano di studi sull'alto medioevo, 1), pp. 219–25.

Irsigler, Franz, 'Mehring. Ein Prümer Winzerdorf um 900', in Duvosquel, Jean-Marie and Thoen, Erik (eds.), *Peasants and Townsmen in Medieval Europe. Studia in Honorem Adriaan Verhulst*, Ghent, 1995, pp. 297–324.

Jacobsen, Werner, 'Die Renaissance der frühchristlichen Architektur in der Karolingerzeit', in Stiegemann, Christoph and Wemhoff, Matthias (eds.), *Kunst und Kultur der Karolingerzeit*, Mainz, 1999, pp. 623–43.

Jankuhn, Herbert, Schlesinger, Walter and Steuer, Heiko (eds.), *Vor- und Frühformen der europäischen Stadt im Mittelalter*, 2 vols., Göttingen, 1975 (Abhandlungen der Akademie der Wissenschaften, Philol.-Histor. Klasse, 3rd series, nos. 83 and 84).

Jankuhn, Herbert, Schützeichel, Rudolf and Schwind, Fred (eds.), *Das Dorf der Eisenzeit und des frühen Mittelalters*, Göttingen, 1977 (Abhandlungen der Akademie der Wissenschaften, Philol.-Histor. Klasse, 3rd series, no. 101).

Jankuhn, Herbert, Janssen, Walter, Schmidt-Wiegand, Ruth and Tiefenbach, Heinrich (eds.), *Das Handwerk in vor- und frühgeschichtlicher Zeit*, 2 vols., Göttingen, 1983 (Abhandlungen der Akademie der Wissenschaften, Philol.-Histor. Klasse, 3rd series, nos. 122–3).

Janssen, Walter, 'Gewerbliche Produktion des Mittelalters als Wirtschaftsfaktor im ländlichen Raum', in Jankuhn et al. (eds.), *Das Handwerk in vor- und frühgeschichtlicher Zeit*, vol. II, pp. 331–47.

Janssen, Walter and Lohrmann, Dietrich (eds.), *Villa–Curtis–Grangia. Landwirtschaft zwischen Loire und Rhein von der Römerzeit zum Hochmittelalter. 16. Deutsch-französisches Historikerkolloquium, Xanten, 1980*, Munich, 1983.

Johanek, Peter, 'Der fränkische Handel der Karolingerzeit im Spiegel der Schriftquellen', in Düwel, Jankuhn, Siems and Timpe (eds.), *Untersuchungen zu Handel und Verkehr*, vol. IV, *Der Handel der Karolinger- und Wikingerzeit*, Göttingen, 1987 (Abhandlungen der Akademie der Wissenschaften, Phil.-Hist. Klasse, 3rd series, no. 156), pp. 7–68.

Kellenbenz, Hermann (ed.), *Handbuch der europäischen Wirtschafts- und Sozialgeschichte*, 6 vols., Stuttgart, 1980.

Kötzschke, R., 'Karl der Grosse als Agrarpolitiker', in *Festschrift Edmund Stengel*, Münster, Cologne, 1952, pp. 181–94.

Kuchenbuch, Ludolf, *Bäuerliche Gesellschaft und Klosterherrschaft im 9. Jahrhundert. Studien zur Sozialstruktur der Familia der Abtei Prüm*, Wiesbaden, 1978.

'Probleme der Rentenentwicklung in den klösterlichen Grundherrschaften des frühen Mittelalters', in Lourdeaux and Verhelst (eds.), *Benedictine Culture*, pp. 130–72.

Grundherrschaft im früheren Mittelalter, Idstein, 1991.

Lauranson-Rosaz, Ch., *L'Auvergne et ses marges (Vélay, Gévaudan) du VIIIe au XIe siècles*, Le Puy-en-Vélay, 1987.

Lebecq, Stéphane, *Marchands et navigateurs frisons du haut moyen âge*, 2 vols., Lille, 1983.

'The Role of Monasteries in the Systems of Production and Exchange of the Frankish World Between the Seventh and the Ninth Centuries', in Hansen and Wickham (eds.), *The Long Eighth Century*, pp. 123–39.

Lesne, Emile, *Histoire de la propriété ecclésiastique en France*, 6 vols., Lille, 1943.

Lohrmann, Dietrich, 'La croissance agricole en Allemagne au Haut Moyen Âge', in *La croissance agricole* (= Flaran 10), pp. 103–15.

Lombard, Maurice, 'Les bases monétaires d'une suprématie économique. L'or musulman du VIIe au XIe siècle', *Annales. Economies–Sociétés–Civilisations* 2 (1947), pp. 143–160.

'Mahomet et Charlemagne. Le problème économique', *Annales. Economies–Sociétés–Civilisations* 3 (1948), pp. 188–99.

Loseby, Simon T., 'Marseille and the Pirenne Thesis II: "Ville Morte"', in Hansen and Wickham (eds.), *The Long Eighth Century*, pp. 167–93.

Lourdeaux, W. and Verhelst, D. (eds.), *Benedictine Culture 750–1050*, Leuven, 1983.

Lyon, Bryce, *The Origins of the Middle Ages. Pirenne's Challenge to Gibbon*, New York, 1972.

Matheus, M. (ed.), *Weinbau zwischen Maas und Rhein in der Antike und im Mittelalter*, Trier, 1997 (Trierer Historische Forschungen 23).

McKitterick, Rosamond (ed.), *The New Cambridge Medieval History*, vol. II, *c. 700–c. 900*, Cambridge, 1995.

Melard, Ludo, 'Millen. Van natuurlandschap tot cultuurlandschap', *Volkskunde* 87 (1986), pp. 262–345.

Ménager, Léon-R., 'Considérations sociologiques sur la démographie des grands domaines ecclésiastiques carolingiens', in *Etudes d'histoire du droit canonique dédiées à Gabriel Le Bras*, 2 vols., Paris, 1965, vol. II, pp. 1317–35.

Mertens, Joseph R., 'Sporen van Romeins kadaster in Limburg?', *Limburg* 37 (1958), pp. 1–7, reprinted in *Acta Archaeologica Lovaniensia* 25(1986).

Metcalf, D. M., 'The Prosperity of North-Western Europe in the Eighth and Ninth Centuries', *Economic History Review* 20 (1967), pp. 344–57.

'A Sketch of the Currency in the Time of Charles the Bald', in Gibson and Nelson (eds.), *Charles the Bald*, pp. 65–97.

Metz, Wolfgang, *Das Karolingische Reichsgut*, Berlin, 1960.

Montanari, Massimo, *La faim et l'abondance. Histoire de l'alimentation en Europe*, Paris, 1995.

Moreland, John, 'Concepts of the Early Medieval Economy', in Hansen and Wickham (eds.), *The Long Eighth Century*, pp. 1–34.

Morimoto, Yoshiki, 'Essai d'une analyse du polyptyque de l'abbaye de St. Bertin (milieu du ixe siècle)', *Annuario Instituto Giapponese di Cultura* 8 (1970–1), pp. 31–53.

'Etat et perspectives des recherches sur les polyptyques carolingiens', *Annales de l'Est* 5–40 (1988), pp. 99–149.

'Autour du grand domaine carolingien: aperçu critique des recherches récentes sur l'histoire rurale du Haut Moyen Âge (1987–92)', in Verhulst and Morimoto (eds.), *Economie rurale et urbaine*, pp. 25–79.

'L'assolement triennal au haut Moyen Age. Une analyse des données des polyptyques carolingiens', in Verhulst and Morimoto (eds.), *Economie rurale et urbaine*, pp. 91–125.

Morrison, Karl F., 'Numismatics and Carolingian Trade: A Critique of the Evidence', *Speculum* 38 (1963), pp. 61–73.

Näsman, Ulf, 'Exchange and Politics: The Eighth–Early Ninth Century in Denmark', in Hansen and Wickham (eds.), *Long Eighth Century*, pp. 35–68.

Nelson, Janet L., *Charles the Bald*, London, 1992.

Noël, René, 'Pour une archéologie de la nature dans le Nord de la "Francia', in *L'ambiente vegetale nell'alto medioevo*, Spoleto 1990 (Settimane di studio del Centro italiano di studi sull'alto medioevo 37), pp. 763–820.

'Moines et nature sauvage: dans l'Ardenne du haut moyen âge', in Duvosquel, Jean-Marie and Dierkens, Alain (eds.), *Villes et campagnes au moyen âge. Mélanges Georges Despy*, Liège, 1991, pp. 563–97.

Patze, Hans and Schwind, Fred (eds.), *Ausgewählte Aufsätze von W. Schlesinger 1965–1979*, Sigmaringen, 1987.

Perrin, Charles-Edmond, 'De la condition des terres dites "ancingae"', in *Mélanges Ferdinand Lot*, Paris, 1925, pp. 619–40.

Phalip, B., 'La charte dite de Clovis', *Revue de la Haute-Auvergne* 1988, pp. 567–607; 1989, pp. 671–96.

Pirenne, Henri, 'Mahomet et Charlemagne', *Revue belge de philologie et d'histoire* 1 (1922), pp. 77–86.

'Un contraste économique: Mérovingiens et Carolingiens', *Revue belge de philologie et d'histoire* 2 (1923), pp. 223–35.

Mohammed and Charlemagne, New York, 1939; paperback edition by Barnes and Noble, New York, 1955.

Platelle, Henri, *Le temporel de l'abbaye de Saint-Amand des origines à 1340*, Paris, 1962.

Querrien, A., 'Parcellaires antiques et médiévaux du Berry', *Journal des Savants* (1994), pp. 235–366.

Raepsaet, Georges, 'The Development of Farming Implements between the Seine and the Rhine from the Second to the Twelfth Centuries', in Astill and Langdon (eds.), *Medieval Farming*, pp. 41–68.

Renard, Etienne, 'Lectures et relectures d'un polyptyque carolingien (Saint-Bertin 844–859)', *Revue d'histoire ecclésiastique* 94 (1999), pp. 392–406.

'La gestion des domaines d'abbaye aux viiie–xe siècles', *De la Meuse à l'Ardenne* 29 (1999), pp. 117–50.

'Les *mancipia* carolingiens étaient-ils des esclaves? Les données du polyptyque de Montier-en-Der dans le contexte documentaire du ixe siècle', in Corbet (ed.), *Les moines du Der*, pp. 179–209.

Rivers, Theodore J., 'Seigneurial Obligations and "Lex Baiuvariorum" I, 13', *Traditio. Studies in Ancient and Medieval History, Thought and Religion* 31 (1975), pp. 336–43.

'The Manorial System in the Light of the Lex Baiuvariorum', *Frühmittelalterliche Studien* 25 (1991), pp. 89–95.

Roblin, M., *Le terroir de Paris aux époques gallo-romaine et franque*, second edition, Paris, 1971.

Rösener, Werner, 'Zur Struktur und Entwicklung der Grundherrschaft in Sachsen in karolingischer und ottonischer Zeit', in Verhulst (ed.), *Le grand domaine*, pp. 173–207.

'Strukturformen der adeligen Grundherrschaft in der Karolingerzeit', in Rösener (ed.), *Strukturen der Grundherrschaft*, pp. 158–67.

Rösener Werner (ed.), *Strukturen der Grundherrschaft im frühen Mittelalter*, Göttingen, 1989.

Rovelli, Alessia, 'Some Considerations on the Coinage of Lombard and Carolingian Italy', in Hansen and Wickham (eds.), *Long Eighth Century*, pp. 195–223.

Sato, Shoichi, 'L'*agrarium*: la charge paysanne avant le régime domanial, vie–viiie siècles', *Journal of Medieval History* 24 (1998), pp. 103–25.

Schlesinger, Walter, 'Die Hufe im Frankenreich', in Patze and Schwind (eds.), *Aufsätze Schlesinger*, pp. 587–614.

Schwarz, G. M. 'Village Populations According to the Polyptyque of the Abbey of St Bertin', *Journal of Medieval History* 11 (1985), pp. 31–41.

Schwind, Fred, 'Beobachtungen zur inneren Struktur des Dorfes in karolingischer Zeit', in Jankuhn, Schützeichel and Schwind (eds.), *Dorf der Eisenzeit*, pp. 444–93.

'Zu karolingerzeitlichen Klöstern als Wirtschaftsorganismen und Stätten handwerklicher Produktion', in Fenske, Rösener and Zotz (eds.), *Festschrift Fleckenstein*, pp. 101–3.

Slater, Terry R. (ed.), *Towns in Decline AD 100–1600*, Aldershot, 2000.

Slicher van Bath, Bernard H., 'The Economic and Social Conditions in the Frisian Districts from 900 to 1500', *AAG Bijdragen* 13(1965), pp. 97–133.

'Le climat et les récoltes en haut moyen âge', in *Agricoltura e mondo rurale in Occidente nell'alto medioevo*, Spoleto, 1966 (Settimane di Studio del Centro italiano sull'alto medioevo 13), pp. 399–425.

Spek, Theo, 'Die bodenkundliche und landschaftliche Lage von Siedlungen, Äckern und Gräberfeldern in Drenthe (nördliche Niederlande)', *Siedlungsforschung* 14 (1996), pp. 95–193 (with an English summary).

Sprandel, Rolf, *Das Eisengewerbe im Mittelalter*, Stuttgart, 1968.

Staab, Franz, 'Aspekte der Grundherrschaftsentwicklung von Lorsch vornehmlich aufgrund der Urbare des Codex Laureshamensis', in Rösener (ed.), *Strukturen der Grundherrschaft*, pp. 305–34.

Steensberg, Axel, 'Agrartechnik der Eisenzeit und des frühen Mittelalters', in Beck, Denecke and Jankuhn (eds.), *Untersuchungen zur eisenzeitlichen und frühmittelalterlichen Flur*, II, pp. 55–76.

Steuer, Heiko, 'Der Handel der Wikingerzeit zwischen Nord- und Westeuropa aufgrund archäologischer Zeugnisse', in Düwel, Jankuhn *et al.* (eds.), *Untersuchungen zu Handel und Verkehr*, IV, *Handel der Karolinger- und Wikingerzeit*, pp. 113–97.

'Gewichtsgeldwirtschaften im frühgeschichtlichen Europa', in Düwel, Jankuhn *et al.* (eds.), *Untersuchungen*, IV, *Handel Karolingerzeit*, pp. 405–527.

Stiegemann, Christoph and Wemhoff, Matthias (eds.), *Kunst und Kultur der Karolingerzeit*, Mainz, 1999.

Tits-Dieuaide, Marie-Jeanne, 'Grands domaines, grandes et petites exploitations en Gaule mérovingienne', in Verhulst (ed.), *Le grand domaine*, pp. 23–50.

Toubert, Pierre, 'L'Italie rurale aux VIIIe–IXe siècles. Essai de typologie domaniale', in *I problemi dell'Occidente nel secolo VIII*, Spoleto, 1973 (Settimane di studio del Centro italiano di studi sull'alto medioevo 20), pp. 95–132.

'Il sistema curtense: la produzione e lo scambio interno in Italia nei secoli VIII, IX e X', in *Storia d'Italia. Annali 6: Economia naturale, economia monetaria*, Turin, 1983, pp. 5–63.

'Le moment carolingien (VIIIe–Xe siècle)', in Burguière, Klapisch-Zuber *et al.* (eds.), *Histoire de la famille*, vol. I, pp. 333–59.

'La part du grand domaine dans le décollage économique de l'Occident (VIIIe–Xe siècles)', in *La croissance agricole* (Flaran 10), pp. 53–86.

Tulippe, Omer, *L'habitat rural en Seine-et-Oise. Essai de géographie du peuplement*, Paris, Liège, 1934.

Van Es, W., 'Dorestad Centred', in Besteman, Bos and Heidinga (eds.), *Medieval Archaeology*, pp. 151–82.

Van Werveke, Hans, 'Comment les établissements religieux belges se procuraient-ils du vin au haut moyen âge?', *Revue belge de philologie et d'histoire* 2 (1923), pp. 643–62, reprinted in Van Werveke, *Miscellanea Mediaevalia*, pp. 12–29.

Miscellanea Mediaevalia, Ghent, 1968.

Vercauteren, Fernand, 'Monnaie et circulation monétaire en Belgique et dans le Nord de la France du VIe au XIe siècle', in *Moneta e scambi nell'alto medioevo*, Spoleto, 1961 (Settimane di studio del centro italiano di studi sull'alto medioevo, 8), pp. 279–311.

Verhein, Klaus, 'Studien zu den Quellen zum Reichsgut der Karolingerzeit', *Deutsches Archiv für Erforschung des Mittelalters* 10 (1954), pp. 313–94 and 11 (1955), pp. 333–92.

Verhulst, Adriaan, 'Karolingische Agrarpolitik: Das *Capitulare de Villis* und die Hungersnöte von 792/93 und 805/06', *Zeitschrift für Agrargeschichte und Agrarsoziologie* 13 (1965), pp. 175–89, reprinted in Verhulst, *Rural and Urban Aspects*, no. VI.

Histoire du paysage rural en Flandre, Brussels, 1966.

'Das Besitzverzeichnis der Genter Sankt-Bavo-Abtei von ca. 800 (Clm 6333)', *Frühmittelalterliche Studien* 5 (1971), pp. 193–234.

'La genèse du régime domanial classique en France au haut moyen âge', in *Agricoltura e mondo rurale in Occidente nell'alto medioevo*, Spoleto, 1966 (Settimane di studio del Centro italiano di studi sull'alto medioevo 13), pp. 135–60 reprinted in Verhulst, *Rural and Urban Aspects*, no. I.

'La diversité du régime domanial entre Loire et Rhin à l'époque carolingienne' in Janssen and Lohrmann (eds.), *Villa-Curtis-Grangia*, pp. 133–48, reprinted in Verhulst, *Rural and Urban Aspects*, no. III.

'Le paysage rural en Flandre intérieure: son évolution entre le IXe et le XIIIe siècle', *Revue du Nord* 62 (1980), pp. 11–30, reprinted in Verhulst, *Rural and Urban Aspects*, no. VIII.

'Etude comparative du régime domanial classique à l'est et à l'ouest du Rhin à l'époque carolingienne', in *La croissance agricole* (Flaran 10), pp. 87–101, reprinted in Verhulst, *Rural and Urban Aspects*, no. IV.

'Settlement and Field Structures in Continental North-West Europe from the Ninth to the Thirteenth Centuries', *Medieval Settlement Research Group. Annual Report* 13 (1998), pp. 6–13.

The Rise of Cities in North-West Europe, Cambridge, 1999.

'Roman Cities, *Emporia* and New Towns', in Hansen and Wickham (eds.), *Long Eighth Century*, pp. 105–20.

Rural and Urban Aspects of Early Medieval Northwest Europe, Aldershot, 1992.

(ed.), *Le grand domaine aux époques mérovingienne et carolingienne. Actes du colloque international Gand 1983*, Ghent, 1985.

Verhulst, Adriaan and Morimoto, Yoshiki (eds.), *L'économie rurale et l'économie urbaine au Moyen Âge*, Ghent, Fukuoka, 1994.

Verhulst, Adriaan and Semmler, Josef, 'Les statuts d'Adalhard de Corbie de l'an 822', *Le Moyen Age* 68 (1962), pp. 91–123 and 233–69.

Verlinden, Charles, *L'esclavage dans l'Europe médiévale*, 1, *Péninsule ibérique-France*, Bruges, 1955 (Rijksuniversiteit Gent.Werken Fac. Letteren en Wijsbegeerte 119).

'A propos de la place des Juifs dans l'économie de l'Europe occidentale aux IXe et Xe siècles', in *Storiografia e Storia, Studi in onore di Eugenio Dupré Theseider*, Rome, 1974, pp. 21–37.

Le vigneron, la viticulture et la vinification en Europe occidentale au moyen âge et à l'époque moderne, Auch, 1991 (Flaran 11).

Violante, Cinzio, *La società milanese nell'età precommunale*, new edition, Rome, Bari, 1974.

Waterbolk, H. T., 'Patterns of the Peasant Landscape', in *Proceedings of the Prehistoric Society* 61 (1995), pp. 1–36.

Weidinger, Ulrich, 'Untersuchungen zur Grundherrschaft des Klosters Fulda in der Karolingerzeit', in Rösener (ed.), *Strukturen der Grund-herrschaft*, pp. 247–65.

Untersuchungen zur Wirtschaftsstruktur des Klosters Fulda in der Karolingerzeit, Stuttgart, 1991.

Weinberger, Stephen, 'Peasant Households in Provence: ca 800–1100', *Speculum* 48 (1973), pp. 247–57.

White, Lynn, Jr, *Medieval Technology and Social Change*, Oxford, 1962.

Wickham, Chris, 'European Forests in the Early Middle Ages: Landscape and Land Clearance', in Wickham, *Land and Power*, pp. 156–61.

Land and Power. Studies in Italian and European Social History, 400–1200, London, 1994.

Wood, Ian, 'Before or After Mission. Social Relations across the Middle and Lower Rhine in the Seventh and Eighth Centuries', in Hansen and Wickham (eds.), *The Long Eighth Century*, pp. 149–66.

Zerner, Monique, 'La population de Villeneuve-Saint-Georges et Nogent-sur-Marne au IXe siècle d'après le polyptyque de Saint-Germain-des-Prés', *Annales de la Faculté des Lettres et des Sciences Humaines de Nice* 37 (1979), pp. 17–24.

'Sur la croissance agricole en Provence', in *La croissance agricole* (Flaran 10), pp. 153–67.

Zerner-Chardavoine, Monique, 'Enfants et jeunes au IXe siècle. La démographie du polyptyque de Marseille 813–814', *Provence Historique* 31 (1988), pp. 355–77.

Added at proof: the author was unable to make use of an important book by Michael McCormick, *Origins of the European Economy: Communications and Commerce AD 300–900*, Cambridge, 2001, as it was published after this book was written.

INDEX

—————— • ——————

Kaupang, 109–10
Kiev, 112
Kissingen, 78, 82
Koblenz, 79, 109
Koningsforeest, 13
Kootwijk, 77
Kordel, 83
Kortrijk, 13
kouter, 18, 19
Krefeld, 77
Kuchenbuch, L., 47

ladmen, 73
Lamprecht K, 2
Langres, 50, 90
Languedoc, 14, 20
Laon, 102
Lebecq, S., 75, 111
Leie river, 13, 18, 19, 101
Lek river, 92, 95
Le Mans, 21, 48
Leo III, pope, 135
Leuven, 13
Lex Baiuwariorum, 36
lidus, 46, 55
Liège, 55
lignare, 50
Lille, 32, 64–5
Limonta, 57
Limousin, 52, 54
Linz, 99
Lion, 104
Liutprand, king of Lombards, 99
Lobbes abbey, 6, 37, 49, 62, 68, 73, 84
Loire, 1, 13, 34, 44, 53, 81, 94, 98, 113,
    121–2, 134
Lombard, M., 3, 118
Lombard kingdom, 73, 99, 104–6, 108
Lombardy, 34
London, 8, 103, 109–10
Lorch, 111
Lorraine, 81–2
Lorsch abbey, 12, 15, 22, 27, 42, 76–7,
    79, 80
Loseby, S., 104
Lotharingia, 81
Lotharius, emperor, 106, 134
Louis the German, king, 89
Louis the Pious, emperor, 51, 98, 119,
    122–3, 130, 133–4
Lucca, 36
luminarii, 51

lunarii, 51
Lyon, 21, 98, 105

Maastricht, 91, 93, 98, 101, 119, 134
Mabompré, 63
Mâconnais, 26
Magdeburg, 111
Main river, 32, 70, 100, 113
Maine, 28, 34
Mainz, 91, 98, 100, 109
maior, 52, 89
Maire, 74
Mälar lake, 109
Majorca, 104
mancipium, 31, 50, 52, 55–6
manopera, 50
manor, 32
    bipartite structure, 33–4, 37
    demesne, 17, 20, 33, 36, 41–3
    demesne-centred, 35, 51–2
    fiscus, 12, 32, 43, 75
    gynaeceum, 74–5
    maior, 52, 89
    ministerium, 77
    non-classical forms, 49–57
    non-tenants, 51
    palatium, 32
    proportion demesne-holdings, 42–3
    rent-collecting type, 55
    royal manor, 32, 39, 40, 56, 75–6
    villicus, 89
mansionilis, 14, 32
mansus, 16, 25, 43–5, 51, 53–4, 57
    charges, 45–9
    half manses, 58
    mansus absus, 58
    mansi carroperarii, 67
    mansus indominicatus, 17, 50
    mansus ingenuilis, 47–8, 50, 56–8
    mansus integer, 51
    mansus lidilis, 56
    mansi manoperarii, 67
    mansus servilis, 43, 46–7, 55–6, 74, 77,
        79
    payments in kind/money, 48–9
    deliveries of wooden objects, 84
    regularity, 51–2
Mantua, 99, 120
market, 89–90, 129–30
    control, 90
    legitimate market, 99
    local market, 97

Ruhr river, 46
Russians, 112

Saale river, 56, 111
Sabina, 14
saga, 73
St Amand abbey, 74, 82–3
St Bavo's abbey, 6, 22, 66, 101
St Bertin abbey, 6, 23, 27, 34, 36, 37,
    41, 43–5, 47, 51–2, 58, 68–9, 73,
    84, 111
St Denis abbey, 16, 17, 22, 68, 74, 82, 98,
    102, 105
St Gall abbey, 34, 68, 72, 73, 75–9, 107, 111
St Germain-des-Prés abbey, 6, 13, 14, 16,
    17, 23, 24, 27, 32, 34, 37–9, 40–2, 45,
    47, 49, 50, 57, 59, 60, 63, 67–9, 70,
    77, 79, 94, 101–2, 134
St Goar, 103
St Hubert, 97
St Martin de Tours abbey, 53, 94
St Maur-des-Fossés abbey, 6, 37, 49, 67, 84
St Maximin abbey, 89
St Mesmin de Micy abbey, 81
St Omer, 51, 69
St Pantaleon chapter, 80
St Peter's abbey, Ghent, 13, 14, 17, 66, 84
St Pierre-le-Vif abbey, 53
St Remi de Rheims abbey, 6, 23, 37, 47–9,
    59, 62–3, 65, 68, 77, 94
St Riquier abbey, 22, 72
St Vaast abbey, 22, 90
St Victor de Marseilles abbey, 23, 25, 37,
    104–5, 134
St Wandrille abbey, 39, 68, 76
salt
    culina, 80
    production, 80–2
    trade, 98–9
Santa Giulia of Brescia abbey, 68, 78, 99
San Vincenzo al Volturno abbey, 72–3, 83
Saragossa, 105
Saran, 80
Sardinia, 104
sar(i)ciles, 73
satio, 63
Saxons, 105
Saxons (Anglo-), 102, 104, 109
Saxony, 42–3, 49, 55–6
Scandinavia, 3, 82, 92, 103, 108–9, 112–13
Sceldeholt, 13
Schaffhausen, 77

Scheldt river, 13, 19, 28, 80, 101, 134
Schleswig, 92
Schwartz, G. M., 27
scindulae, 50
sedile, 91
Seine river, 5, 34, 37, 94, 98, 101–2, 109,
    113, 134
Septimer, pass, 106
services, 35–7, 45–9
    carriage (*carropera*), 50, 67
    handwork (*manopera*), 50, 67
    noctes, 46–7, 56
    ploughing (*aratura, corvada*), 50, 67
    tillage (*beneficia*), 50
    transport, 50, 59, 60
    see also ancinga, riga
servus, 46, 55–7
sessus, 91
sheep, 66
Sicily, 105
silk, 107, 112
silver, 3
Sint-Martens-Latem, 18
slaves, 35, 36, 43, 46–7, 53, 105
    slave trade, 4, 105, 107, 112
Slavs, 105, 111–12
Slicher van Bath, B.H., 64
smith, 77
    ferrarii ministeriales, 79
Soignes, forêt de, 13
Soissons, 102
Sologne, 13
Somme river, 98
sortes (absentes), 36, 58
Southampton, 92, 109
Spain, 105–6, 112
    Muslim, 112
    northern, 52
    see also Catalonia
spices, 3, 107, 112
Spoleto, 14
Staffelsee, 42, 43, 46, 56, 75
Stavelot-Malmedy abbey, 12
strata legittima, 94, 99
sunken huts, 74
swords, 84, 110

tasca, 53
Taunus, 12
technique (agricultural)
    fallow system, 61
    olive oil, 3, 107

Index

Cambridge Medieval Textbooks

Already published

Germany in the High Middle Ages *c.* 1050–1200
HORST FUHRMANN

The Hundred Years War
England and France at War *c.* 1300–*c.* 1450
CHRISTOPHER ALLMAND

Standards of Living in the Later Middle Ages:
Social Change in England, *c.* 1200–1520
CHRISTOPHER DYER

Magic in the Middle Ages
RICHARD KIECKHEFER

The Papacy 1073–1198: Continuity and Innovation
I. S. ROBINSON

Medieval Wales
DAVID WALKER

England in the Reign of Edward III
SCOTT L. WAUGH

The Norman Kingdom of Sicily
DONALD MATTHEW

Political Thought in Europe 1250–1450
ANTONY BLACK

The Church in Western Europe from the Tenth
to the Early Twelfth Century
GERD TELLENBACH
Translated by Timothy Reuter

The Medieval Spains
BERNARD F. REILLY

England in the Thirteenth Century
ALAN HARDING

Monastic and Religious Orders in Britain 1000–1300
JANET BURTON

Religion and Devotion in Europe *c.* 1215–*c.* 1515
R. N. SWANSON

Medieval Russia, 980–1584
JANET MARTIN

The Wars of the Roses: Politics and the Constitution in England,
c. 1437–*c.* 1509
CHRISTINE CARPENTER

The Waldensian Dissent: Persecution and Survival, *c.* 1170–*c.* 1570
GABRIEL AUDISIO
Translated by Claire Davison

The Crusades, *c.* 1071–*c.* 1291
JEAN RICHARD
Translated by Jean Birrell

Medieval Scotland
A. D. M. BARRELL

Roger II of Sicily: A Ruler between East and West
HUBERT HOUBEN
Translated by Graham A. Loud and Diane Milburn

The Carolingian Economy
ADRIAAN VERHULST

Medieval Economic Thought
DIANA WOOD

Other titles are in preparation